The *Rifftionary*

One Hundred & Thirty-Two
of the world's most famous guitar riffs
from
The Ace Of Spades
to
Ziggy Stardust

Published 2004
© International Music Publications Ltd
International Music Publications Ltd is a Faber Music company
Bloomsbury House
74–77 Great Russell Street
London WC1B 3DA

Text and research by Simon Troup
Compiled by James Sleigh
New arrangements, engraving and book layout by Artemis Music Ltd.
www.artemismusic.com
Design by Dominic Brookman

Printed in England by Caligraving Ltd
All rights reserved

ISBN10: 0-571-52521-0
EAN13: 978-0-571-52521-8

Reproducing this music in any form is illegal and forbidden by the Copyright, Designs and Patents Act, 1988

To buy Faber Music publications or to find out about the full range of titles available,
please contact your local music retailer or Faber Music sales enquiries:

Faber Music Ltd, Burnt Mill, Elizabeth Way, Harlow, CM20 2HX England
Tel: +44(0)1279 82 89 82   Fax: +44(0)1279 82 89 83
sales@fabermusic.com   fabermusic.com

THE MUSIC SHOP
£11·99

D1330431

Contents

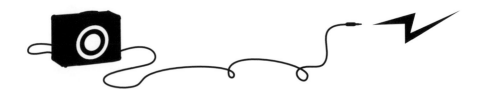

Contents

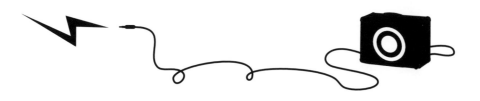

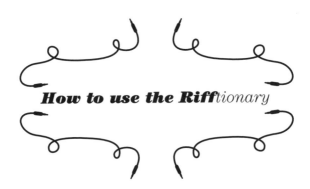

How to use the Rifftionary

Read this before attempting to Riff

This book includes a huge selection of riffs, from metal shredding to hard rock classics, from funk licks to jazz and beyond. In each case we've tried to notate the riff in the simplest way, so you can get riffing as quickly as possible.

If the riff is based around a chord sequence (like *Lust For Life* – see page 73) then we've used chord diagrams to show how the riff progresses. Simply strum in the appropriate rhythm and follow the chord changes. See below for a brief explanation of how to use chord diagrams.

Most of the riffs are shown in guitar tablature (or **TAB** for short). Don't worry if you can't read music – by listening to the original recording and referring to the **TAB**, you should be able to play any of the riffs in this book.

How to use chord diagrams

Chord diagrams represent the neck of the guitar, viewed vertically – the horizontal lines in the box represent the frets and the vertical lines represent the strings. The bottom (thickest) string is shown on the left and the top (thinnest) string is shown on the right.

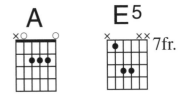

The blobs on the chord diagram tell you where to put your fingers. An '**x**' at the top of the box tells you not to play that string and an '**o**' tells you to play an open string. That's all there is to it!

If the chord is played higher up the neck then the position of the lowest fret used is shown to the right of the chord box.

*How to use the **Riff**tionary*

How to use TAB

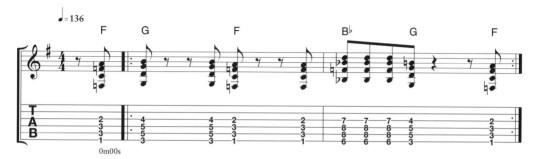

Guitar **TAB** is your key to the world of riffs.

Ignore the musical notes for the time being and look at the lower part of the music example, where the word 'TAB' is written vertically. The six horizontal lines stretching across the page represent the six strings of your guitar.

The bottom line represents the bottom E string (the thickest string) and the top line represents the top E string (the thinnest string). The numbers on each string tell you at which fret the string should be pressed down. So, in the example above, to play the first chord of the riff, you need to fret the bottom string at the first fret, the fourth and fifth strings at the third fret, and the third string at the second fret. That's basically all you need to know.

On page 6, you'll find an explanation of some of the most commonly used symbols, which indicate specific guitar techniques like slides, hammer-ons, pull-offs etc.

If the guitar is specially tuned this is indicated at the beginning of the TAB stave (see *Beautiful People* – page 17). If the guitar needs to be tuned down to match the original recording this is also indicated.

> "
> Guitar
> **TAB**
> *is your key to the world of*
> **Riffs**
> "

Guitar TAB Glossary

Bending Notes

  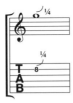  

Half Step:
Play the note and bend string one half step.*

Whole Step:
Play the note and bend string one whole step.

Quarter-tone Bend:
Play the note and bend string slightly to the equivalent of half a fret.

Prebend (Ghost Bend):
Bend to the specified note, before the string is picked.

Prebend And Release:
Bend the string, play it, then release to the original note.

Tremolo Bar

Muting

Unison Bend:
Play both notes and immediately bend the lower note to the same pitch as the higher note.

Specified Interval:
The pitch of a note or chord is lowered to a specified interval and then may or may not return to the original pitch. The activity of the tremolo bar is graphically represented by peaks and valleys.

Muted Strings:
A percussive sound is made by laying the fret hand across all six strings while pick hand strikes specified area (low, mid, high strings).

Articulations

Hammer On:
Play lower note, then "hammer on" to higher note with another finger. Only the first note is attacked.

Pull Off:
Play higher note, then "pull off" to lower note with another finger. Only the first note is attacked.

Palm Mute:
The note or notes are muted by the palm of the pick hand by lightly touching the string(s) near the bridge

Legato Slide:
Play note and slide to the following note. (Only first note is attacked)

*A half step is the smallest interval in Western music; it is equal to one fret. A whole step equals two frets.

Words and music by:
Marc Bolan

From the album:
Most artists use singles as a means of promoting albums. Curiously, this song didn't appear on the album *Tanx*, which was also released in 1973, but has been included on numerous compilation albums following Marc's death in a car accident in 1977.

Highest chart placing (UK):
4 (1973)

Highest chart placing (US):
102 (1973)

Guitarist:
Marc Bolan

How to get that sound:
This track needs an old British valve amp such as an Orange or Marshall set for mid crunch (gain 6/10) and a Gibson Les Paul with the bridge pickup selected.

Fascinating fact:
A Fender Telecaster previously owned by Marc Bolan was used extensively by Mike Oldfield during the recording of *Tubular Bells*.

Technical tips:
If you're wondering why the low E string bends sound a little thin, it's because they're doubled by a bass guitar on the original recording.

Most memorable lyric:
Friends say it's fine, friends say it's good
Everybody says it's just like Rock 'n' roll
I move like a cat, talk like a rat, sting like a bee
Babe I'm gonna be your man.

© 1973 Wizard (Bahamas) Ltd, Surrey CR0 7JR

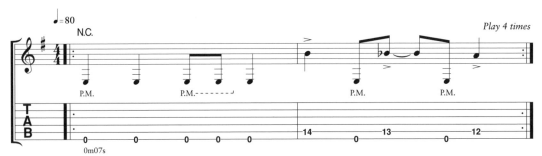

Words and music by:
Ian Kilmister, Edward Clarke and Philip Taylor

From the album:
Ace Of Spades (1980)

Highest chart placing (UK):
15 (1980)

Set-up:
Fender Stratocaster through a Marshall stack

Guitarist:
'Fast' Eddie Clarke

How to get that sound:
Use the bridge pickup with 10/10 volume and tone, lots of gain and drive the power amp hard, don't bother with any effects and stand well back.

Fascinating fact:
'Fast' Eddie was just one of the five guitarists who have played in Motorhead since they formed in 1975. The album *Ace Of Spades* (from which this track is taken) was Motorhead's highest charting album, getting as high as number 4 in the UK album chart. The band were in a category of their own – their gigs at this time were attended by as many punks as rockers – one minute they were recording with The Damned, the next they were on tour with Ozzy Osbourne. Lemmy even recorded a version of Tammy Wynette's 'Stand By Your Man' with Wendy O. Williams and The Plasmatics.
Rumour has it that Lemmy hates the song and has been singing 'The eight of spades' in protest for some years – he claims that no-one has ever noticed.

Technical tips:
Don't be confused by the intro – Lemmy opens with four bars of overdriven Rickenbacker bass and Fast Eddie begins the guitar riff just after the snare build up by drummer Phil 'Philthy Animal' Taylor.

Most memorable lyric:
You know I'm born to lose
And gambling's for fools
But that's the way I like it baby
I don't wanna live for ever.

'Motorhead are supposed to to make people wonder what's the next bad thing that will happen to them. Life is about brief periods of bliss followed by terrible long periods of depression, angst and brutality.' Lemmy

© 1980 Motor Music Ltd, London WC2H 0QY

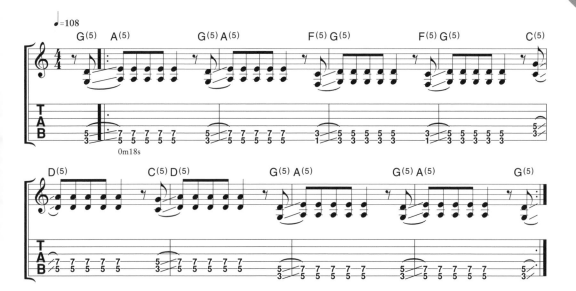

Words and music by:
Robert Palmer

From the album:
Riptide (1985)

Highest chart placing (UK):
5 (1986)

Highest chart placing (US):
1 (1986)

Guitarist:
Andy Taylor (Duran Duran/Power Station)

How to get that sound:
The rhythm guitar sound is very reminiscent of 1980s Z.Z.Top, and isn't difficult to reproduce on most modern amps. Set the amp gain to about 8/10 for a solid distortion sound and then shape the tone with the amp tone controls, or better still, use a parametric or graphic E.Q. You should aim for a middly tone, so don't go overboard on treble or presence.
Use a guitar with powerful humbucking pickup, such as a Super Strat.

Fascinating fact:
Chaka Khan was going to duet with Robert on this track but had to pull out at the last minute for contractual reasons.

Technical tips:
Carefully mute the rests between each phrase with the side of your picking hand, the riff will lose definition if you don't. You can also add the occasional whammy bar vibrato on the last note of each phrase, but don't overdo it.

Most memorable lyric:
You like to think that you're
Immune to the stuff, oh yeah
It's closer to the truth to say
You can't get enough
You know you're gonna have to face it
You're addicted to love

© 1985 Bungalow Music, USA Warner/Chappell North America Ltd, London W6 8BS

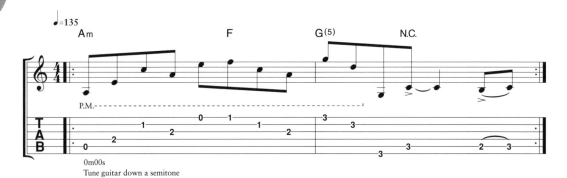

0m00s
Tune guitar down a semitone

Words and music by:
Edward Van Halen, Alex Van Halen, Michael Anthony and David Lee Roth

From the album:
Van Halen (1978)

Guitarist:
Eddie Van Halen

Set-up:
In his early career Eddie bought a custom Stratocaster type guitar body and neck from a local guitar maker and assembled a guitar himself. He then added a Gibson P.A.F. pickup because he liked the sound produced by a Les Paul but didn't like the shape. Other parts were added from a host of other makers, and Eddie dubbed the guitar the 'Frankenstrat'. He favoured Marshall amplifiers and cabinets, usually run flat out (See page 36 - 'Eruption').

How to get that sound:
You'll need to add some delay and phaser effects to get an authentic sound. Select the bridge pickup only, preferably a high output humbucker, and dial in plenty of preamp gain (9/10).

Fascinating fact:
Van Halen used to add a clause (or 'rider') in their contracts with venues that stated they expected a bowl of M&M candies to be made available for the band in the dressing room, with all of the brown ones removed. The band claim that it was used as a way of checking whether the venue management had bothered to read the contract. If the M&Ms weren't in the dressing room, or if they found any brown M&Ms in the bowl, then the management had probably also ignored safety aspects such as power requirements and safe working load of the stage (no doubt to carry the enormous weight of Eddie's vast number of speaker cabinets!). Failing to pass the M&M test would usually result in a laborious point by point check of all requirements, and very occasionally resulted in the cancellation of a show if the venue wasn't up to scratch.

Technical tips:
The palm mute is executed by resting the side of your picking hand lightly on the strings right next to the bridge. Make sure that you get a clear contrast between the palm muted arpeggios and the unmuted ending, which should be heavily accented.

Most memorable lyric:
You know you're semi-good lookin'
And on the streets again
Ooh yeah, you think you're really cookin' baby
You better find yourself a friend, my friend.

© 1984 Van Halen Music and Diamond Dave Music, USA
Warner/Chappell Music Ltd, London W6 8BS and Chrysalis Music Ltd, London W10 6SP

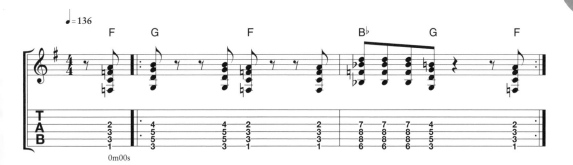

Words and music by:
Raymond Davies

From the album:
Kinks-Size (1964)

Highest chart placing (UK):
2 (1964)

Highest chart placing (US):
7 (1964)

Guitarist:
Dave Davies

Set-up:
Harmony Meteor through a 'customised' Elpico amplifier

How to get that sound:
The Harmony Meteor is a semi acoustic with the familiar hollow twang you'd expect from such an instrument. The more difficult part of this particular equation is the Elpico amp, long discontinued and very, very rare now. If you *can* get your hands on one, you then need the audacity to set about the speaker with a razor blade, cutting through the cone several times as Dave did (for research purposes!).

Fascinating fact:
The Kinks believe that they were nearly murdered by the notorious serial killer John Wayne Gacy, who confessed to killing over 30 people and burying them in a small crawl space beneath his house. He acted as a promoter for one of The Kinks' concerts in Illinois and invited the band back to his house following the concert. They excused themselves and left despite his protestations after only a few drinks as they felt something was odd about the situation.

Technical tips:
Part of the delight of Dave's playing is that it's rude and crude – he's probably the original punk rocker. Get the sound right and then just knock it out.

Most memorable lyric:
I believe that you and me last forever
Oh yeah, all day and night I'm yours
Leave me never
The only time I feel alright is by your side
Girl I want to be with you all of the time.

© 1964 Edward Kassner Music Co Ltd, London SW6 6SE

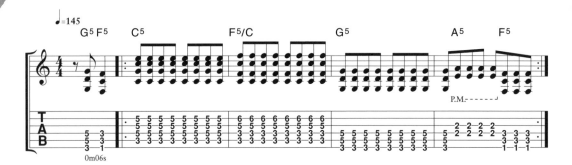

Words and music by:
Mark Hoppus and Tom DeLonge

From the album:
Enema Of The State (2000)

Guitarist:
Tom DeLonge

Set-up:
Fender Stratocaster

How to get that sound:
Select the neck pickup and set the preamp gain to about 7/10 for a clean mid crunch. Warm the sound up by adding a little more bass and middle than usual and add some reverb (2/10) for ambience.

Fascinating fact:
Blink 182 used to be known just as Blink but added the 182, a number selected at random, for legal reasons as there was another band already recording under the name Blink.

Technical tips:
Open crunchy rhythm playing like this (especially the F5/C chord, for example) can sound terrible if you don't tune accurately – use a digital tuner if necessary.

Most memorable lyric:
Keep your head still
I'll be your thrill
The night will go on
My little windmill.

'We were bored and we couldn't get chicks. So we decided if we were in a band, that would take care of two problems at once.' Tom

© 1999 Fun With Goats, USA
EMI Music Publishing Ltd, London WC2H 0QY

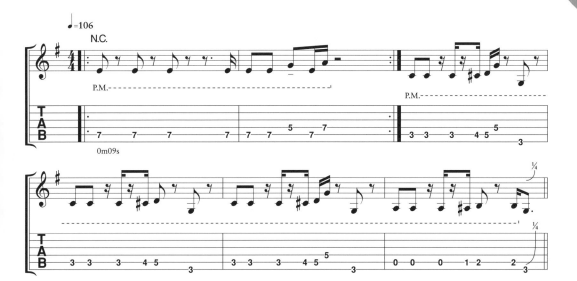

Words and music by:
John Deacon

From the album:
The Game (1980)

Highest chart placing (UK):
7 (1980)

Highest chart placing (US):
1 (1980)

Guitarist:
Brian May

Set-up:
Self-made guitar and Vox AC30 amplifiers

How to get that sound:
Everything about Brian May's guitar sound is unusual, if not unique. First of all there's his guitar, the 'Red Special'. He made it himself with some help from his father, using amongst other things an old mahogany fireplace and some blockboard. This is fed into a device which acts as a treble booster. It too is home made and Brian describes it as "very primitive".

For amplification Brian uses three carefully positioned AC30s, each one fed with a different combination of signal and effects – just another part of the alchemy in producing his signature guitar sound.

Please remember to ask for parental consent before taking a hatchet to your own fireplace, or better still, buy the Guild signature model which is being used more and more by Brian nowadays as as a backup for 'Red Special'.

Most memorable lyric:
There are plenty of ways
That you can hurt a man
And bring him to the ground
You can beat him
You can cheat him
You can treat him bad
You can leave him when he's down.

© 1980 Queen Music Ltd, London WC2H 0QY

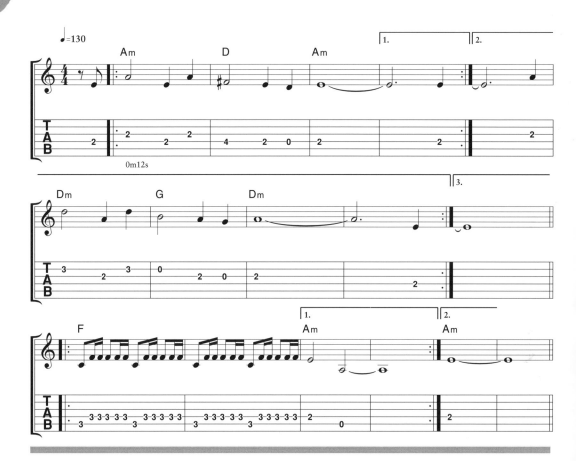

Music by:
Jerry Lordan

Highest chart placing (UK):
1 (1960)

Guitarist:
Hank Marvin

Set-up:
Fender Stratocaster through Vox AC15/AC30

How to get that sound:
The Stratocaster/AC30 combination should be fairly easy to emulate, especially as the AC30 is modelled in so many 'virtual' guitar effects units such as the Line 6 Pod. The only tricky addition for the sake of authenticity would be a Watkins (Wem) Copycat tape echo unit. Connoisseurs will try to convince you that all the noise and tape flutter was a *good* thing.

Fascinating fact:
This was The Shadows' first number one hit, and stayed at the top of the charts in the UK for 21 weeks.

© 1959 Francis Day & Hunter Ltd, London WC2H 0QY

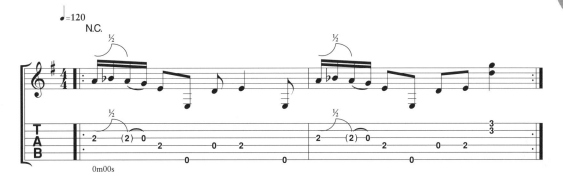

Words and music by:
Lenny Kravitz and Craig Ross

From the album:
Are You Gonna Go My Way? (1992)

Highest chart placing (UK):
4 (1993)

Guitarist:
Lenny Kravitz

Set-up:
Gibson Les Paul and Marshall Stack

How to get that sound:
Use the bridge pickup and set the amp for plenty of distortion (8/10). There's very little other treatment, so add only a little reverb (2/10) and shape the sound a little with the amp tone controls.

Fascinating fact:
Lenny grew up in Hollywood and attended Beverly Hills High School along with Slash, the guitarist from Guns 'n' Roses.
Lenny's mother, Roxie Roker, is an actress, best known for her starring role in *The Jeffersons*. He was married for six years to actress Lisa Bonet who starred in *The Cosby Show*, and more recently Lenny has been dating Nicole Kidman.
Aside from producing his own material he has had great success as a producer with other artists such as Madonna, for whom he both wrote and produced 'Justify My Love', and Vanessa Paradis.

Technical tips:
Use your second and third fingers together to play the opening bend – it's a tricky one because of the high string tension at the second fret caused by its proximity to the nut. Careful use of damping will prevent the notes ringing together – aim to make the phrases sound like a single fluid line.

Most memorable lyric:
So tell me why we got to die
And kill each other one by one
We've got to love and rub-a-dub
We've got to dance and be in love.

© 1992 Miss Bessie Music and Wigged Music, USA
EMI Virgin Music Ltd, London WC2H 0QY and Warner/Chappell Music Ltd, London W6 8BS

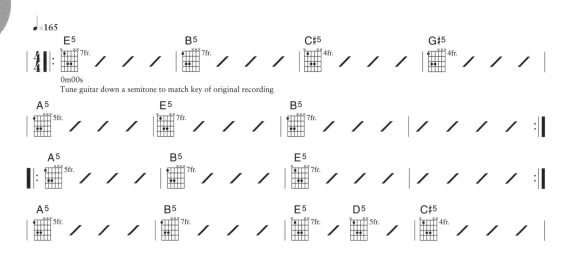

♩=165

Tune guitar down a semitone to match key of original recording

---

Words and music by:
Billy Armstrong, Frank Wright and Michael Pritchard

From the album:
Dookie (1994)

Guitarist:
Billie Joe Armstrong

Set-up:
Fernandes Stratocaster copy through a Marshall Stack

How to get that sound:
This sound is easy to emulate on most guitar/amp combinations by choosing the bridge pickup and setting the amp for 'crunch' (gain at about 7/10) instead of saturated distortion. Add a little reverb for ambience (2/10). Finally, shape the tone with the tone controls on the amplifier.

Fascinating fact:
'Green day' is a slang term which means spending the entire day hanging out with friends and smoking marijuana, and is the title of one of the tracks on their first album *39/Smooth*. The album was recorded in only one day for less than $1,000.

Technical tips:
The trick in this song is to get the palm muting and accented 'stabs' coordinated well, while making slick movements from one power chord to the next. You should aim to get some warmth out of the chords by muting only lightly.

Most memorable lyric:
I went to a shrink
To analyze my dreams
She says it's lack of sex
That's bringing me down.

I went to a whore
He said my life is a bore
And quit my whining
'Cause it's bringing her down.

© 1994 Green Daze Music, USA
Warner/Chappell North America Ltd, London W6 8BS

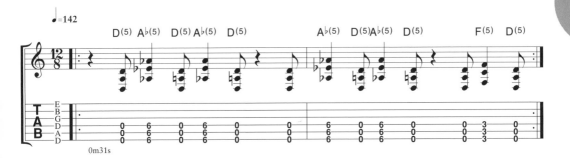

Words and music by:
Marilyn Manson and Twiggy Ramirez

From the album:
Antichrist Superstar (1996)

Highest chart placing (UK):
18 (1997)

Guitarist:
Twiggy Ramirez

How to get that sound:
Any guitar with a high output humbucker can be used to emulate this guitar sound. Use the bridge pickup in combination with a saturated overdrive (set the amplifier gain to 10/10). The guitars are recorded almost completely dry (without reverb).

Fascinating fact:
Marilyn Manson (real name Brian Warner) is a Reverend of the Church Of Satan. This 'honour' was bestowed on him by the founder of the San Francisco-based society, Anton LaVey. Manson is not the only celebrity to have been inducted into the 'church', he follows in the footsteps of Sammy Davis Jr, Jayne Mansfield and Kim Novak.
Manson's music, along with that of the German group Rammstein, was cited as an influencing factor in the Columbine High School tragedy in 1999, in which two teenage gunmen killed 12 students and a teacher before killing themselves. Some time later it came to light that police searches of the boys' homes failed to reveal any interest in either Manson or his music. Manson subsequently issued a terse attack on the media and religious groups who had seized on the tragedy as an excuse to attack him and his music. The events echo a similar case in which the group Judas Priest were taken to court in 1990 (and eventually acquitted) for influencing two teenagers to commit suicide in 1985 through subliminal messages on the *Stained Class* album.

Technical tips:
Note that the low E string is tuned down a tone to D ('Drop D tuning'). Use the open D string as a reference, or use a chromatic tuner.

Most memorable lyric:
The beautiful people
The beautiful people
It's all relative to the size of your steeple
You can't see the forest for the trees,
And you can't smell
Your own sh** on your knees.

© 1996 Dinger And Ollie Music, Songs Of Golgotha Music and Blood Heavy Music, USA
EMI Music Publishing Ltd, London WC2H 0QY

B

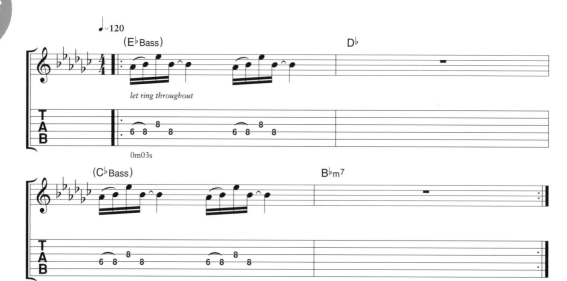

Words and music by:
Lindsey Buckingham

From the album:
Tango In The Night (1987)

Highest chart placing (UK):
9 (1987)

Highest chart placing (US):
5 (1987)

Guitarist:
Lindsey Buckingham

Set-up:
Gibson Chet Atkins

How to get that sound:
If you don't have a Gibson Chet Atkins guitar to hand, use an acoustic guitar or an electric with a clean tone. Play fingerstyle, and 'pull' the strings slightly to get a little snap in the tone.

Fascinating fact:
Lindsey often doubles guitar parts with a banjo, and this can be heard in the chorus section of this song. He's also well known for his 'Travis picking', a fingerstyle technique employing the thumb to play alternating bass notes on the lower three strings while the index and middle fingers play syncopated notes on the upper three strings. This is demonstrated in 'The Chain' which appears on page 119.

Most memorable lyric:
You said that you love me
And that you always will
Oh, you begged me to keep you
In that house on the hill
Looking out for love
Big, big love.

© 1987 Now Sounds Music, USA
EMI Music Publishing Ltd, London WC2H 0QY

Words and music by:
Michael Jackson

From the album:
Thriller (1982)

Highest chart placing (UK):
1 (1983)

Highest chart placing (US):
1 (1983)

Fascinating fact:
Thriller is the biggest selling album of all time, with sales topping 53 million copies internationally. Six songs from the album made their way into the top ten of the singles charts, and to date the album has been certified as 25 times platinum.

Technical tips:
The guitar parts shown here are arrangements of the bass guitar and keyboard parts. Play the parts separately by playing only the notes with the stems up, or only the notes with the stems down. If you're really adventurous – play _all_ the notes! The finger numbers shown are there only for those brave enough to combine both parts. Try not to play the chords too staccato – listen to the synth parts on records for reference. This is going to require some deft left-hand work!

Set-Up:
On the original recording these are keyboard synthesizer parts, but most guitar synths will have voices which closely match. If you have a guitar synth with a split point function, set the lower part to operate up to F# (4th fret) on the D (4th) string – everything above that should be the upper chord voice.

Most memorable lyric:
And mother always told me
Be careful of who you love
And be careful of what you do
'Cause the lie becomes the truth.

© 1982 Mijac Music, USA
Warner/Chappell Music Ltd, London W6 8BS

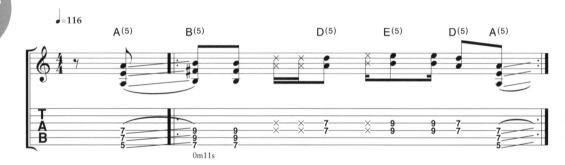

Words and music by:
Huddie Ledbetter

From the album:
Ram Jam (1977)

Highest chart placing (UK):
7 (1977)

Highest chart placing (US):
18 (1977)

Guitarist:
Bill Bartlett

How to get that sound:
Don't go overboard with the distortion, set the gain to about 7/10 if you have single coil pickups, 6/10 for humbuckers. The tone is fairly 'vintage', if you have modelling effects try using some of the Fender 'black face' presets.

Fascinating fact:
When 'Black Betty' was released it proved to be quite controversial, with some groups claiming that it was racist. It seems to have escaped the protester's notice that the writer, Leadbelly, was a black American folk singer and guitarist, but somehow it's adoption by Ram Jam wasn't deemed palatable.
The song was re-released in 1990, climbing as high as number 13 in the singles chart. More recently it has been covered by Tom Jones, and to this day the Ram Jam recording remains popular in clubs and on juke boxes.
On the internet, the song is often wrongly credited as being by Nazareth in file sharing programs (not that we indulge ourselves!), possibly because Bartlett's vocals are similar to Dan McCafferty's.

Technical tips:
This is a very funky rhythm part that demands fluid and accurate strumming. Use a medium to light pick, and ensure the muted notes (played by momentarily relaxing fretting hand pressure on the strings) don't become blurred by other notes ringing on.

Most memorable lyric:
Black Betty had a child
Bam a lam
The damn thing gone wild
Bam a lam
She said I'm worrying out of mind
Bam a lam
The damn thing gone blind
Bam a lam.

© 1939 Folksways Music Publishers Inc, USA
Kensington Music Ltd, London SW10 0SZ

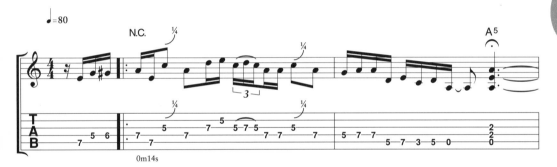

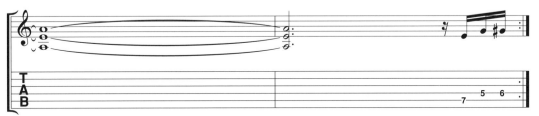

Words and music by:
Jimmy Page, Robert Plant and John Paul Jones

From the album:
" " (a.k.a. *Led Zeppelin IV*) (1971)

Highest chart placing (US):
15 (1972)

Guitarist:
Jimmy Page

Set-up:
Gibson Les Paul, Marshall Stack & Roger Mayer Tonebender fuzz box

How to get that sound:
This rhythm guitar features the unmistakeable sound of a fuzz box, which generates a more aggressive clip than can be achieved by overdriving the Marshall alone. Select the bridge pickup on the guitar and dial in enough fuzz effect to create a noticeable clip without ruining the basic tone.

Fascinating fact:
Urban legend relates that the band's name came from a comment from Keith Moon (drummer for The Who) who told Jimmy Page that the band would "... go down like a f***ing lead balloon". This

is contested by John Entwistle (bass player for The Who) who claims that he had planned to use the name Led Zeppelin for a project of his own, and mentioned it to someone who went on to become the band's production manager.

Technical tips:
This riff is based around an A minor pentatonic scale at the 5th fret. Be careful not to bend the quarter tones into semitones or you'll lose the bluesy feel.

Most memorable lyric:
Hey, hey, baby
When you walk that way
Watch your honey drip
Can't keep away.

© 1972 Superhype Publishing Inc, USA
Warner/Chappell Music Ltd, London W6 8BS

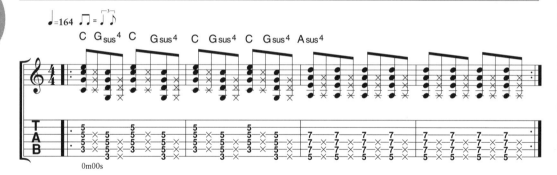

Words and music by:
Jack White

From the album:
Elephant (2003)

Guitarist:
Jack White

Set-up:
Airline through a Sears Silvertone 100 watt

How to get that sound:
The distortion here is at the top end of the crunch scale, so set the gain to about 8/10. Much of the rest of the sound is created by strumming hard.
The Airline guitar used by Jack is not exactly a professional model, and you may get better results by putting down the $5,000 P.R.S. that took you five years to save up for, and using that old plank of a guitar that your parents bought for you all those Christmases ago.

Fascinating fact:
The album *Elephant*, completed in only two weeks, was recorded in a tiny London studio, crammed full of vintage recording equipment. The tracks were recorded to 8 track analogue reel to reel tape, a far cry from the modern trend of recording digitally to hard disc. Jack wanted the recording equipment itself to create a retro feel for the album, and openly questions the approach used by many bands – spending vast amounts of money and month after month in the recording studio.
One of the songs on the album, 'Ball And Biscuit', is named after a vintage STC 4021 microphone that was used in the recording of the album, and which is shaped very much like its nickname.

Technical tips:
Don't spend too long trying to nail the muted notes, they're really only the result of releasing the strings to get to the next chord. This is 'attitude' rock, it's more about feel than technical execution – you'll ruin the riff if you play it too prettily.

Most memorable lyric:
Don't you think that I'm bound to react now?
My fingers definitely turning to black now
Maybe I'll put my love on ice
And teach myself, maybe that'll be nice.

'I'm not a technically proficient guitar player. I'm about what it means at the moment, the attack of it and the attitude.' Jack White

© 2003 Peppermint Stripe Music, USA
EMI Music Publishing Ltd, London WC2H 0QY

Words and music by:
Jon Lord, Ritchie Blackmore, Ian Gillan, Roger Glover and Ian Paice

Highest chart placing (UK):
2 (1970)

Highest chart placing (US):
66 (1970)

From the album:
Originally appeared only as a single.

Guitarist:
Ritchie Blackmore

Set-up:
Fender Stratocaster through a Marshall Stack

How to get that sound:
This is a classic Stratocaster/Marshall combo – the gain (7/10) shouldn't be so high that it disguises the single coil pickup tone from the guitar.

Fascinating fact:
Ritchie's first Stratocaster was given to him, indirectly, by Eric Clapton in 1970 (before that date he played a Gibson ES-335) – "Eric Clapton had given it to one of our roadies, who gave it to me. The instrument had a fantastic sound, but the intonation was out. Finally I realised I was going to have to go out and buy a new one."
The solo features some of the wildest whammy bar abuse on record, something that could only sensibly be attempted in the studio, coming as it does nine years before the locking tremolo system. Floyd Rose cited Ritchie as a major influence in his creation of the locking tremolo system.

Technical tips:
Although entirely pentatonic, many players will be in unfamiliar territory playing E minor pentatonic in this position. However, it's worth getting to know, as many of the older school players such as Jimi Hendrix, Ritchie Blackmore, Jimmy Page and Stevie Ray Vaughan used it.

Most memorable lyric:
I don't need a dark tree
I don't want a rough sea
I can't feel
I can't see
Maybe I'll find on the
Way down the line
That I'm free
Free to be me
Black night is a long way from home.

© 1970 B Feldman & Co Ltd trading as Hec Music, London WC2H 0QY

Words and music by:
Brian Welch, David Silveria, Jonathan Davis, James Shaffer, Reginald Arvizu, Denis Shin and Chuck Ryan

From the album:
Korn (1994)

Guitarist:
Brian 'Head' Welch
James 'Munky' Shaffer

Set-up:
Ibanez 7, 12 and 14 string signature guitars through Mesa Boogie amplifiers.

How to get that sound:
For the Gtr. 1 part use minimal distortion (gain 5/10) and an Electro Harmonix Small Stone phaser. The first entry of Gtr. 2 is a little more distorted but completely dry (without reverb). The main riff uses a Big Muff distortion pedal, although much of the intensity comes from the fact that the notes are so much lower than a regular six string.

Fascinating fact:
Much of Korn's unique sound is down to their use of seven string guitars. Popular myth holds that these were 'invented' by Steve Vai, but as long ago as 1969 Gretch were producing the seven string 'Van Eps', an early signature model named after and created for the jazz legend George Van Eps, who used the extra low B string to play independent bass lines against chords on the upper strings.

Technical tips:
Korn tuned their guitars down a tone, and tuned the extra 7th string to A, giving the following tuning (low to high):

A D G C F A D

The transcription above is for a regular six string guitar in standard tuning with the low E string tuned down to A (use the open A 5th string as reference). No doubt purists will complain, but for everyone else, we've saved you the price of a new guitar and a couple of hours worth of tuning problems bringing the whole thing back up to pitch again afterwards.

Most memorable lyric:
There's a place inside my mind
A place I like to hide
You don't know the chances
What if I should die?

© 1995 Goat Head Music, Jolene Cherry Music, Sex Art Publishing and Abba-Cadaver Music, USA
Warner/Chappell North America Ltd, London W6 8BS and Bug Music Ltd, London W14 0LJ

Words and music by:
Freddie Mercury

From the album:
A Night At The Opera (1975)

Highest chart placing (UK):
1 (1975)

Highest chart placing (US):
9 (1976)
2 (1992)

Guitarist:
Brian May

Set-up:
Self made guitar and Vox AC30 amplifiers

How to get that sound:
(See page 13 – 'Another One Bites The Dust')

Fascinating fact:
Brian doesn't use a pick, he's always used old sixpences. They're no longer legal tender in the UK, but Brian has steadfastly refused to go metric despite stringent EU legislation. Faced with the dilemma of ever dwindling stocks of sixpences Brian had the Royal Mint strike a batch featuring his own silhouette on one side, solving the problems of personalised plectra and the sixpence shortage at a stroke. Hurrah!

Technical tips:
There should be no real difficulties here, although the syncopated rhythm may catch you out if you're not very familiar with the track.

Most memorable lyric:
I see a little silhouetto of a man
Scaramouch, scaramouch
Will you do the fandango
Thunderbolt and lightning
Very very frightening me
Gallileo (Gallileo)
Gallileo (Gallileo)
Gallileo Figaro
Magnifico!

© 1975 B Feldman & Co Ltd trading as Trident Music Ltd, London WC2H 0QY

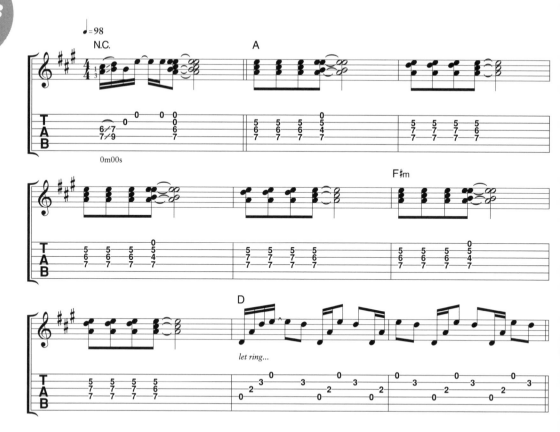

Words and music by:
Chrissie Hynde and James Honeyman-Scott

From the album:
The Pretenders (1980)

Highest chart placing (UK):
1 (1979)

Highest chart placing (US):
14 (1980)

Guitarist:
James Honeyman-Scott

Set-up:
Zemantis guitar

How to get that sound:
Select the guitar's bridge pickup and use a totally clean tone on the amplifier. Add a little delay, chorus and reverb.

Fascinating fact:
Tragedy struck The Pretenders twice early on in their career when, in 1982 at the age of only 25, James Honeyman-Scott died of a heroin and cocaine overdose. Ironically, Pete Farndon, the band's bass player, had been sacked from the band only two days earlier, and also died of an overdose in 1983.
Johnny Marr (guitarist for The Smiths and The The) has called James Honeyman-Scott "the last important influence on my playing before I went out on my own".

Most memorable lyric:
Gonna use my arms
Gonna use my legs
Gonna use my style
Gonna use my sidestep
Gonna use my fingers
Gonna use my, my, my imagination.

© 1979 EMI Music Publishing Ltd trading as Clive Banks Songs, London WC2H 0QY

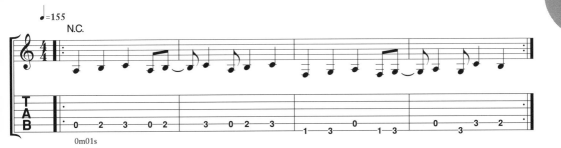

Words and music by:
Kenneth Downing, Robert Halford and Glenn Tipton

From the album:
British Steel (1980)

Highest chart placing (UK):
12 (1980)

Guitarists:
Glenn Tipton
K.K. Downing

Set-up:
Fender Stratocaster through a Marshall stack

How to get that sound:
Select the bridge pickup on the guitar and set the gain to 8/10 to distort but not completely saturate.

Fascinating facts:
Where do we start? At the top of the rock tree since the early 70s, Judas Priest have caused sensational headlines on a number of occasions. In 1978 Priest's singer Rob Halford was stopped from using a bullwhip in his Top Of The Pops performance because of the protestations of Donnie and Marie Osmond, who were on the same bill. In 1980 the group paid £50,000 ransom to recover master tapes of the British Steel album after they were stolen from a New York recording studio. Later that year Rob Halford dropped his trousers and underpants in front of the entire audience of the Rainbow Theatre in London. In 1990 they were caught up in the infamous 'subliminal message' trial (see page 17 – 'Beautiful People').

More recently their ability to write catchy anthems has gained them followers in the 2D world, where 'Breaking The Law' is Beavis and Butthead's all-time favourite air guitar track, and Otto, the bus driver from *The Simpsons*, always appears to be listening to 'Living After Midnight' on his headphones.

Technical tips:
This is the riff played by Glenn Tipton on record. It's very straight forward – just make sure that your muting is up to the job and remember to bang your head on the down beats.

Most memorable lyric:
Breaking the law, breaking the law
Breaking the law, breaking the law
Breaking the law, breaking the law
Breaking the law, breaking the law

© 1980 Geargate Ltd, Ebony Tree Ltd and Crewglen Ltd
EMI Songs Ltd, London WC2H 0QY

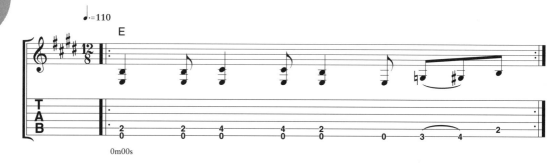

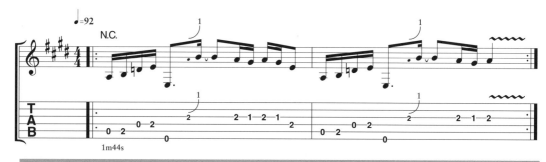

Words and music by:
Willie Dixon

From the album:
Led Zeppelin II (1969)

Highest chart placing (UK):
1 (1969)

Guitarist:
Jimmy Page

Set-up:
1959 Gibson Les Paul played through a 100-watt Marshall

How to get that sound:
See "Whole Lotta Love" – page 134

Fascinating fact:
Willie Dixon, the writer of this song, accused Led Zeppelin of plagiarism in 1987 over alleged similarities between 'Whole Lotta Love' and his song 'You Need Love'. The case was settled out of court.

Technical tips:
The main two riffs in the song are tabbed out above. The mellower opening section follows a classic blues sequence – when the chord changes just move the fingerboard pattern up one string to match the A chord.

The second section starts at 1m44s and features a bluesy bend at the 2nd fret on the G string. The string tension here is high, so you'll really need to grab hold of it – support your second finger with your index finger if necessary.

Most memorable lyric:
Tried to tell you baby
What you tryin' to do?
Tried to love you baby
Love some other man too

Bring it on home
Bring it on home...

© 1964 Hoochie Coochie Music, USA
Bug Music Ltd, London W14 0LJ

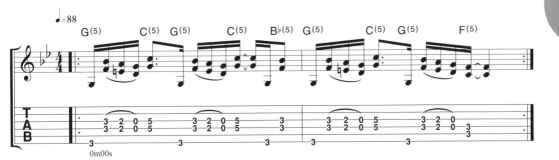

0m00s

Words and music by:

Ritchie Blackmore, Jon Lord, David Coverdale and Ian Paice

From the album:

Burn (1974)

Guitarist:

Ritchie Blackmore

Set-up:

Fender Stratocaster through Marshall Stack

How to get that sound:

Another classic vintage Stratocaster/Marshall combination. Set the gain to 7/10 and select the guitar's bridge pickup.

Fascinating fact:

Burn (the album) was recorded during November 1973 using the Rolling Stones Mobile Studio. Other bands who took advantage of the Mobile Studio include Led Zeppelin (*Led Zeppelin III*) and Bad Company (*Bad Company*).

This album marked the departure of vocalist Ian Gillan to form The Ian Gillan Band, and the arrival of David Coverdale, who went on to great success with Whitesnake.

Technical tips:

This is not an easy riff to play at speed. The combination of fast 16th note pull-offs and the low G note call for some deft fingerwork. Play the low G with your second finger, the first double stop with a third finger partial barre, and the second double stop with a first finger partial barre, the rest should be self explanatory.

Don't allow the low G note to ring on, and stand well clear of the drummer in the verses.

Most memorable lyric:

The sky is red, I don't understand
Past midnight I still see the land
People are sayin' the woman is damned
She makes you burn with a wave of her hand
The city's a blaze, the town's on fire
The woman's flames are reaching higher
We were fools, we called her liar
All I hear is "Burn".

'I've always played every amp I've ever had full up, because rock and roll is supposed to be played loud. Also keeping the amp up is how you get your sustain. I turn down on the guitar for dynamics.' Ritchie Blackmore

© 1974 Deep Purple Music (Overseas) Ltd, Surrey KT4 7BY

29

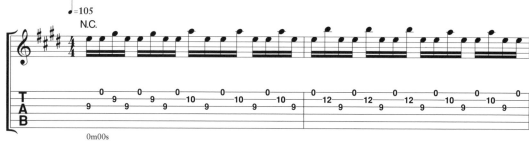

Words and music by:
Martin Coogan

From the album:
Turtle Soup (1991)

Highest chart placing (UK):
18 (1991)
19 (2003)

Guitarists:
Martin Coogan
Martin Glyn Murray

Set-up:
Gibson Les Paul

How to get that sound:
This song needs a good rounded acoustic type tone, so select both bridge and neck pickups on your guitar. Set the gain so that the sound distorts but you can still hear each string ringing on as you play the riff. You've got too much gain if you can't hear each note as it's played. Finally, add a little light reverb and some delay – once again don't go overboard on these effects, just use them to add a little atmosphere.

Fascinating fact:
Martin is the brother of comedian Steve Coogan.

Technical tips:
Let all the notes ring together, being particularly careful not to snag the top string while you're changing the notes on the second. Instead of using a pick, try fingerpicking the notes using your thumb, index and middle finger, this makes it easy to maintain the repeated three string pattern.

Most memorable lyric:
Can you understand me now
I'll get through somehow
You won't ever get me down
Won't see me hanging around.

Can you dig it, oh yeah
Can you dig it, oh yeah
Can you dig it, oh yeah
Can you dig it
What I'm saying?
One little kiss isn't anything
I won't be sad.

© 1990 EMI Virgin Music Ltd, London WC2H 0QY

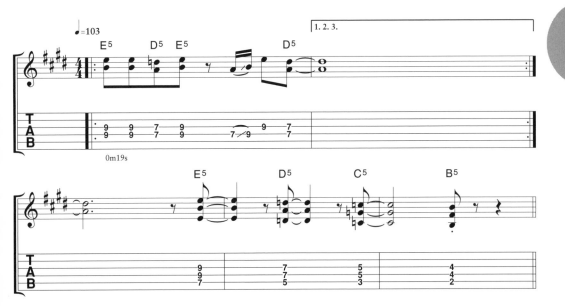

Words and music by:
J.J. Cale

From the album:
Slowhand (1977)

Highest chart placing (UK):
30 (1980)

Guitarist:
Eric Clapton

Set-up:
Fender Stratocaster through a Marshall stack

How to get that sound:
There are many different layered guitars on 'Cocaine', each with a different treatment. For this, the main riff, choose the bridge pickup and setup some mild distortion at the amplifier. Don't add any other effects – like many recordings from this period it's a very dry guitar sound.

Fascinating fact:
In the 60s one of Eric's favourite amplifier settings was to set his Marshall 100 watt SuperLead amplifiers to "full on everything", where all the controls were set to maximum, leaving Eric to make the adjustments at the guitar, where volume

and tone changes could have a dramatic affect on distortion and tone. With this sound he claimed to be able to get the feedback sustain effect "100 miles away".

On a more bizarre note, in 1977 astronomers from Harvard College Observatory discovered and named a planet after Eric. *Clapton* (Minor planet number 4305) is around 400 million kilometers outside of Eric's feedback sustain range.

Most memorable lyric:
If you got bad news
You wanna kick them blues
Cocaine
When your day is done
And you wanna run
Cocaine.
She don't lie, she don't lie, she don't lie
Cocaine.

© 1979 Audigram Music Inc, USA
Warner/Chappell Artemis Music Ltd, London W6 8BS

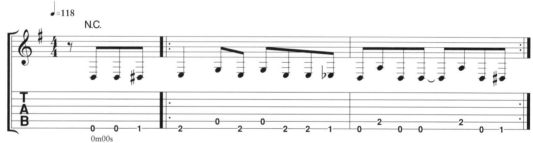

♩=118

N.C.

0m00s

Tune down a tone to match key of original recording

Words and music by:
Kurt Cobain

From the album:
Nevermind (1991)

Highest chart placing (UK):
9 (1992)

Highest chart placing (US):
32 (1992)

Guitarist:
Kurt Cobain

Set-up:
Fender Mustang and Mesa Boogie Studio 22

How to get that sound:
The intro shown here is a very clean sound with a little chorus and reverb added. Cobainophiles should use an Electro-Harmonix Small Clone Chorus; everyone else, use any chorus pedal you like.

Fascinating fact:
Cobain's riffs redefined rock music in the early 90s – they were sharp, focused, and what's more, nearly everyone could play them.

"I took lessons for a week, I learned how to play 'Back In Black' by AC/DC, and it's pretty much the 'Louie Louie' chords, so that's all I needed to know. I never did pay the guitar teacher for that week either, I still owe him money. But that's it, y'know, I just started writing songs on my own once you know the power chord, you don't need to know anything else."

Most memorable lyric:
Come doused in mud
Soaked in bleach
As I want you to be
As a trend
As a friend
As an old memoria
Memoria.

© 1991 The End Of Music and EMI Virgin Songs Inc, USA
EMI Virgin Music Ltd, London WC2H 0QY

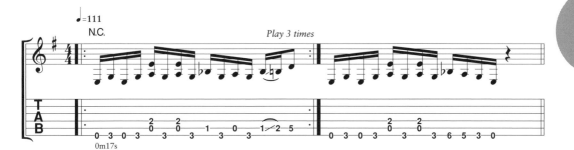

Words and music by:
Vincent Abbott, Darrell Abbott, Rex Brown and Philip Anselmo

From the album:
Cowboys From Hell (1990)

Guitarist:
Darrell 'Dimebag' Abbott

Set-up:
Dean ML electric guitar

How to get that sound:
You'll need a guitar with some very high output humbuckers to get near this tone. Use plenty of gain (as high as 10/10 if necessary) and shape the sound with any available E.Q. – a graphic or parametric E.Q. would be very useful. The tone is very middly, so you won't need a lot of bass.

Fascinating fact:
Dimebags' biggest early influence was Ace Freeley of *Kiss*, so much so that he sports a tattoo of the guitarist.
In his youth, Dimebag was banned from entering State guitar competitions because he had won so many of them.

Technical tips:
Only sheer alternate picking ability is going to get you through this song, and all the standard advice applies. Use a metronome and build up the speed slowly. Try not to let your picking wrist become too tense by trying too hard, if the speed isn't there then grim determination won't work, you'll need to work up to it slowly. Don't give yourself carpal tunnel syndrome, just practise more often.

Most memorable lyric:
Here we come reach for your gun
And you better listen well my friend
You see it's been slow down below
Aimed at you we're the
Cowboys from hell
Deed is done again, we've won
Ain't talking no tall tales friend
'Cause high noon, your doom
Comin' for you we're the
Cowboys from hell.

'When people run into us in a bar, they'll be jumping up and down all over the place, expecting us to be the craziest motherf***ers you'd ever meet – eating glass, drinking everything in sight. I mean, we're like that some days, but you do have to moderate yourself.' Vinnie

© 1991 Power Metal Music Inc and Cota Music Inc, USA
Warner/Chappell Music Ltd, London W6 8BS

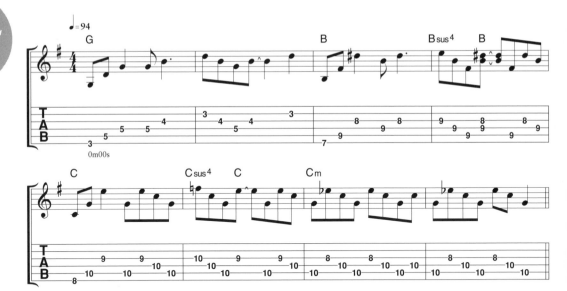

Words and music by:
Thomas Yorke, Edward O'Brien, Colin Greenwood, Jonathan Greenwood, Philip Selway, Albert Hammond and Mike Hazelwood

From the album:
Pablo Honey (1993)

Highest chart placing (UK):
7 (1993)

Highest chart placing (US):
34 (1993)

Guitarists:
Thomas Yorke
Ed O'Brien
Johnny Greenwood

Set-up:
Gibson ES-335 through Vox AC30

How to get that sound:
The most distinctive feature of the guitar sound is the use of tremolo. Ed used a Dunlop TS1 pedal for 'Creep', but it should be very easy to emulate with any tremolo unit. Choose a mixture of both bridge and neck pickups on the guitar and use the clean channel on your amp with a little reverb to create some ambience.

Fascinating fact:
The band used to be called On A Friday because that was the only day of the week they could rehearse together. Just after signing their first recording contract they changed their name to Radiohead, after a song by Talking Heads.

Most memorable lyric:
*I don't care if it hurts, I want to have control
I want a perfect body, I want a perfect soul
I want you to notice, when I'm not around
You're so f***ing special
I wish I was special.*

© 1992 Warner/Chappell Music Ltd, London W6 8BS and Rondor Music (London) Ltd, London W6 8JA

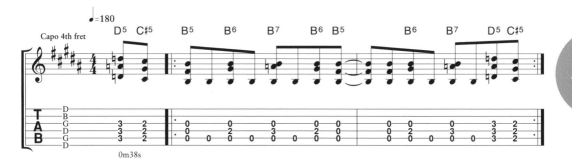

Words and music by:
Francis Rossi and Bob Young

From the album:
On the Level (1975)

Highest chart placing (UK):
1 (1974)

Guitarist:
Francis Rossi
Rick Parfitt

Set-up:
Fender Telecaster through Vox AC30

How to get that sound:
The guitar sounds are fairly typical of what you get simply by plugging a Telecaster into an AC30. If you have a modelling amplifier or effects unit head straight for the AC30 patches.

Fascinating fact:
Within the band Francis Rossi is called *The GOMORR*, which stands for *Grand Old Man Of Rock and Roll*. Rick Parfitt on the other hand, is *The WOMORR* or *Wild Old Man Of Rock and Roll*. Topping them both however is John Coghlan, who is simply known as *Spud*.

Technical tips:
Once you're in tune this song is very straight forward, but tuning to 'Open G' can be tricky. Tune the 6th and 1st strings down to D using the 4th string as your reference, then tune the 5th string down to G using the 3rd string for reference – better still, use a chromatic tuner.

Most memorable lyric:
I have found you out you see
I know what you're doing
What you're doing to me
I'll keep on and say to you
Again again again again again again again
Deeper and down.

'You can't rock on an empty stomach, can you? So we always have a bit of breakfast before we start. It's civilised; get to rehearsals, have breakfast and then get it on.' Rick Parfitt

---

© 1974 EMI Music Publishing Ltd, London WC2H 0QY and Valley Music Ltd, London W6 8JA

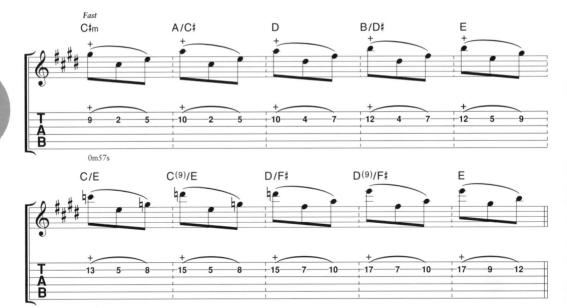

Words and music by:
Edward Van Halen, Alex Van Halen, Michael Anthony and David Lee Roth

From the album:
Van Halen (1978)

Guitarist:
Eddie Van Halen

Set-up:
(See Page 10 - 'Ain't Talkin' 'Bout Love')

How to get that sound:
Eddie used a Univox EC-80 tape echo unit (a.k.a. 'The Brat') and an MXR Phase 90 Phaser for this track. His Marshall Super-Lead 100 watt amp head was run flat out (everything 10/10 – also a trick used by Eric Clapton), but Eddie found that he could control the power output by using an Ohmite Variac variable transformer, getting the tone without the otherwise inevitable feedback problems.

Fascinating fact:
The band had not originally planned to feature a guitar instrumental on the album, but producer Ted Templeman overheard Eddie warming up before a recording session and consequently went on to record it in a single take.

Technical tips:
This is the infamous tapped arpeggio section. Each chord form is shown only once between dashed barlines, but should be repeated ad lib.

Eddie is flat out going for it at this point and doesn't follow any regular repeat pattern (and neither should you!).

For those new to the concept, the tap is a type of hammer-on usually executed by the index finger of the picking hand, and is nearly always followed by a pull-off – simply pull the tapping finger slightly to one side to sound the note below. The note to be played with the fretting hand is indicated with a + sign. Some players prefer to use the middle finger for the tap, that way you don't have to worry about ditching the pick in the middle of a guitar solo.

© 1978 Van Halen Music and Diamond Dave Music, USA
Warner/Chappell Music Ltd, London W6 8BS and Chrysalis Music Ltd, London W10 6SP

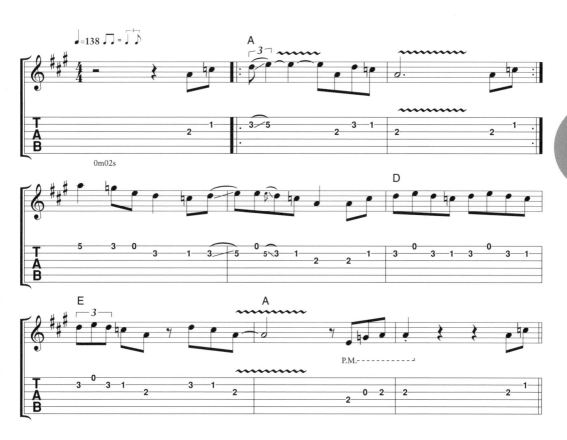

Music by:
Hank Marvin, Bruce Welch and Jet Harris

From the album:
Tracks 1961 (1961)

Highest chart placing (UK):
6 (1961)

Guitarist:
Hank Marvin

Set-up:
Fender Stratocaster through Vox AC15/AC30

How to get that sound:
(See Page 14 - 'Apache')

Fascinating fact:
Hank is commonly thought to be the first owner of a Fender Stratocaster in the UK. He had wanted one since seeing Buddy Holly And The Crickets on their 1958 UK tour and, after failing to find one for sale in the UK, was given one as a present from Cliff Richard who had asked a friend to bring one back from the US.

© 1961 The Shadows Music Ltd, London NW1 8BD

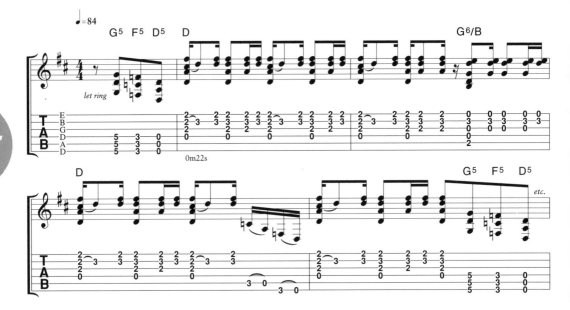

Words and music by:
Brian May

From the album:
Jazz (1978)

Guitarist:
Brian May

Set-up:
Self made guitar and Vox AC30 amplifiers

How to get that sound:
(See Page 13 - 'Another One Bites The Dust')

Fascinating fact:
'Fat Bottomed Girls', penned by Brian May, was released as a double A side single with 'Bicycle Race'. Freddie wrote the latter song shortly after watching the Tour De France, inspired by the sight of so many men on bikes. The two concepts were brought together when the band decided to hold a bicycle race involving 50 naked women, which was duly organised and held at Wimbledon Stadium. First prize in the race was to appear on the cover of the single, which was promptly censored following outrage from some sections of the then more conservative media. Contrary to what you may assume from the title, the young lady featured on the cover of the single has a fantastic

Technical tips:
Don't get hung up on trying to play the exact combination of note groups which are notated, rather take it as a cue for the general style and then work from the recording.

Most memorable lyric:
I was just a skinny lad
Never knew no good from bad
But I knew life before I left my nursery
Left alone with big fat Fanny
She was such a naughty nanny
Heap big woman you made a bad boy out of me
Hey hey!

© 1978 Queen Music Ltd, London WC2H 0QY

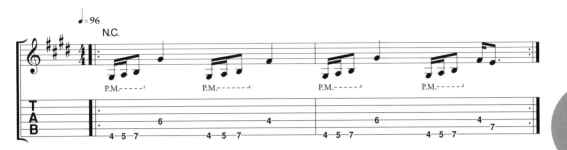

Words and music by:
Greig Nori, Deryck Whibley, Steve Jocz and Dave Baksh

From the album:
All Killer No Filler (2001)

Highest chart placing (UK):
8 (2001)

Highest chart placing (UK):
66 (2001)

Guitarists:
Deryck Whibley
Dave Baksh

Set-up:
Gibson Les Paul through Line 6 POD Pro through Marshall

How to get that sound:
The intro to this track has the warm bass response of a Fender Twin, probably modelled on the POD Pro, fed by the bridge pickup of a Les Paul. It shouldn't be necessary to set the gain much beyond about 6/10.

Fascinating fact:
Dave Baksh's nickname is *Brown Sound*, for the simple reason that, well, he's brown and he makes a lot of sound.
Deryck Whibley's nickname is *Bizzy D*, busy in a sense that he has a very active sex life while on tour with the band. His criminal record covers everything from theft and vandalism to arson.

Technical tips:
Try not to choke the strings completely in the palm muted sections – you can adjust the 'warmth' of the mute according to the pressure that you place on the strings with your palm. The harder you press, and the further away from the bridge, the harder and more brittle the sound will be. Conversely, you can achieve warmer tones and a little more depth by allowing the strings to ring a little, simply by moving closer to the bridge and muting only lightly.

Most memorable lyric:
Well I'm a no goodnick
Lower middle class brat
Back packed and I don't
Give a s*** about nothing.
You be standing on the corner
Talking all that kufuffin.
But you don't make sense
From all the gas you be huffing.

© 2001 Rectum Renovator Music and Chrysalis Music, USA
EMI Music Publishing Ltd, London WC2H 0QY and Chrysalis Music Ltd, London W10 6SP

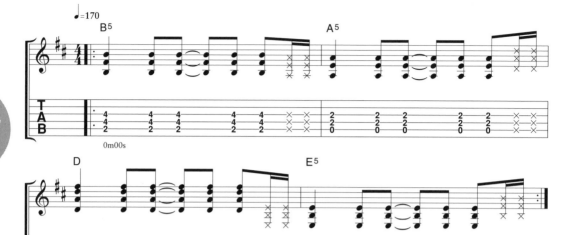

Words and music by:
Jack White

From the album:
White Blood Cells (2001)

Guitarist:
Jack White

Set-up:
Airline through a Sears Silvertone 100 watt

How to get that sound:
Set the gain to 8/10 and select the bridge pickup on the guitar, leaving the tone controls set fully open at 10/10. The track is completely dry, so set the reverb to 0/10.

(See also Page 22 - 'Black Math')

Fascinating fact:
In July 2003 The White Stripes cancelled a whole block of tour bookings after Jack broke his finger in a car accident. Eager to appease fans who had bought tickets for the shows, which included appearances at the 'T in the Park', Witness and Reading festivals, Jack had a video put up at *thewhitestripes.com* showing him undergoing surgery. Strains of 'Seven Nation Army' and 'Black Math' can clearly be heard playing in the

background – just the kind of music a surgeon needs to maintain total concentration while drilling pilot holes into your proximal phalange.

Most memorable lyric:
She turns and says "Are you alright?"
I said "I must be fine cause
My heart's still beating"
She says "Come and kiss me
By the riverside
Bobby says it's fine
He don't consider it cheating".

© 2001 Peppermint Stripe Music, USA
EMI Music Publishing Ltd, London WC2H 0QY

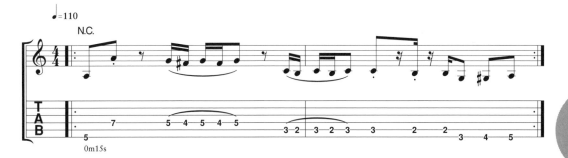

Words and music by:
Ian Brown and John Squire

From the album:
Turns Into Stone (1992)

Highest chart placing (UK):
8 (1992)

Guitarist:
John Squire

Set-up:
Hofner Verithin 335 through a Fender Twin amplifier

How to get that sound:
Use a semi-acoustic guitar set to both bridge and neck pickups. The Fender Twin sound is noted for its warm bass and presence, and is often included in modelling effects units such as the POD or Behringer V-Amp. Don't add too much middle or you'll ruin the woody tones of the semi-acoustic. Reverb is fairly noticeable and should be set at around 4/10.

Fascinating fact:
In March 1990 all four members of The Stone Roses appeared in court charged with criminal damage carried out at the offices of their previous record company, Revolver FM. All four men pleaded guilty to the charges.
The band had poured paint over cars, smashed windows, entered the Revolver offices and thrown blue and white paint over company boss Paul Birch, his girlfriend and most of his office. Their 'artistic' protest had been caused by Revolver re-releasing the single 'Sally Cinnamon' (along with

an accompanying video) without their consent or participation. During the proceedings the band were described as "A group of musicians who call themselves The Stone Roses" much to the amusement of fans attending the trial. Eventually they were fined £3,000 each and resolved to do the same thing again as soon as the commotion died down.

Most memorable lyric:
These boots were made for walking
The Marquis de Sade don't wear no
Boots like these
Gold's just around the corner
Breakdown's coming up round the bend.

'If you think of four Brooke Bond chimps on very strong drugs, then that would be very close to how we were.' Mani

© 1989 Zomba Music Publishers Ltd, London SW6 3JW

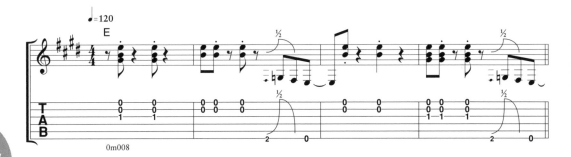

G

0m008

Words and music by:
Marc Bolan

From the album:
Electric Warrior (1971)

Highest chart placing (UK):
1 (1971)

Highest chart placing (US):
10 (1972)

Guitarist:
Marc Bolan

Set-up:
Gibson Les Paul through Dallas Arbiter Fuzz Face

How to get that sound:
Select the bridge pickup on your guitar, turn volume and tone to 10/10 and feed the signal into the Fuzz Face. There's no particular amp tone to strive for here, the character is all in the Fuzz Face. Sculp the sound at the amp into a middly nasal tone and leave it dry. Most fuzz boxes will substitute nicely for the Fuzz Face – it's a very low tech unit.

Fascinating fact:
Spare a thought for Marc's son, Rolan Bolan, who shares his silly name with other rock star children such as Moon Unit and Dweezil Zappa (Frank Zappa), Zowie Bowie (David Bowie) and Heavenly Hiraani Tiger Lily Hutchence (Michael Hutchence). Boomtown Rats vocalist Bob Geldof seems to have topped them all with his trio, Fifi Trixibelle Geldof, Peaches Honeyblossom Geldof and Pixie Geldof.

Technical tips:
Careful palm muting for the staccato chords and a simple semitone bend are all that are required for this riff, which differs little in style to other Marc Bolan classics such as '20th Century Boy' (see page 7).

Most memorable lyric:
You're built like a car
You got a hubcap
Diamond star halo
You're built like a car
Oh yeah.

Get it on
Bang a gong
Get it on.

© 1971 Westminster Music Ltd, London SW10 0SZ

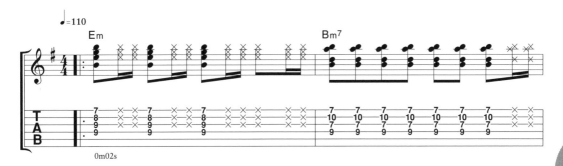

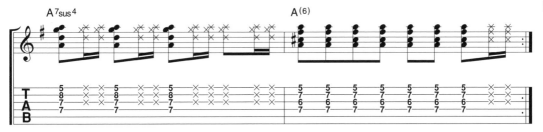

Words and music by:
Bernard Edwards and Nile Rodgers

From the album:
Risqué (1979)

Highest chart placing (UK):
5 (1975)

Highest chart placing (US):
1 (1979)

Guitarist:
Nile Rodgers

Set-up:
Tokai Stratocaster

How to get that sound:
On a Strat with a five position pickup toggle switch, select position two (where position one is 'down' and selects the bridge pickup). On a three position toggle switch you can try the old trick of balancing the switch between positions one and two to get the same 'out of phase' sound. Stratocaster type guitars produce a wide variation of tones from the out of phase settings and you may find that your Strat will sound closer to the track in another position, so experiment a little. Add some compression (2/10) and chorus (as low as 1/10 – just to space the sound a little) and then dial in a very conservative amount of reverb to taste. The rest of the tone is going to be in your ability to play light, tight and funky.

Technical tips:
The difficulty with this type of funk strumming is in getting clear separation between the chords that are strummed and those that are muted. It's all too easy to get half muted chords in between the transitions. Practise the riff slowly, aiming to nail every chord and mute.

Most memorable lyric:
Let's cut the rug
A little jive and jitterbug
We want the best
We won't settle for less
Don't be a drag
Participate
Clams on the half shell and
Roller-skates
Roller-skates.

© 1979 Bernard's Other Music and Sony/ATV Songs LLC, USA
Warner/Chappell Music Ltd, London W6 8BS and Sony/ATV Music Publishing, London W1V 2LP

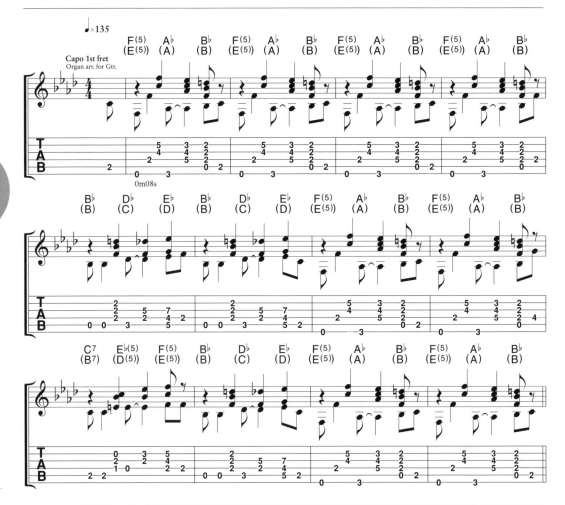

Music by:
Booker T. Jones, Steve Cropper, Al Jackson and Lewie Steinberg

From the album:
Green Onions (1962)

Highest chart placing (UK):
7 (1979)

Highest chart placing (US):
3 (1962)

Guitarist:
Steve Cropper

Fascinating fact:
In 1962, Stax Records house band Booker T & The MG's were in the recording studio waiting for singer Billy Lee Riley to turn up. He didn't, but the band put the time to good use by recording an impromptu jam session based around a standard 12-bar blues they had been playing. It proved to be an instant, albeit unplanned success. Seventeen years later it became a success in the UK when it was included in the film *Quadrophenia*.

Technical tips:
This guitar part is an arrangement of the organ riff as played by Booker T. Most bars consist of three chord shapes, the first two of which are arpeggiated by playing bass notes before the rest of the chord. Learn the chord shapes first as some may be a little unfamiliar. You can lose a lot of the song's impact by playing this too loosely – the devil is most definitely in the detail, so pay attention to the way the chords are arpeggiated, and watch out for tricky passing notes between bars.

© 1962 East Publications Inc, Progressive Music Publishing Co Inc and Unichappell Music Inc, USA. Carlin Music Corp, London NW1 8BD for the Commonwealth of Nations (including Hong Kong but excluding Canada/Australasia), Eire and Israel.

Words and music by:
Alvertis Isbell, Allen Alvoid Jones Jr. and Otis Redding

From the album:
Shake Your Money Maker (1990)

Highest chart placing (US):
39 (1990)

Highest chart placing (US):
45 (1990)

Guitarist:
Rich Robinson
Jeff Cease

Set-up:
Gibson Les Paul through a Fender Twin

How to get that sound:
This is a warm, low tech guitar sound, using only a little gain (5/10) that sits on the very edge of distortion. Select both bridge and neck pickups, and don't ruin the natural woody tone of the instrument through over-enthusiastic tone contouring – keep it simple. If you have digital reverb select a small or medium room setting and add only enough to pull away from a totally dry sound (2/10). If your amplifier has only spring reverb, it may be better not to add it at all.

Technical tips:
Don't be tempted to add vibrato to the long held notes – many players will do this automatically, and as a result, ruin the melodic simplicity.

Most memorable lyric:
Boys come along a dime by the dozen
That ain't nothing but ten cent lovin'
Hey little thing let me light your candle
'Cause mama I'm sure hard to handle, now,
Gets around.

© 1968 (renewed) Irving Music Inc and East Memphis Music Corp, USA
Carlin Music Corp, London NW1 8BD for the Commonwealth of Nations (including Hong Kong but excluding Canada/Australasia) and Eire.

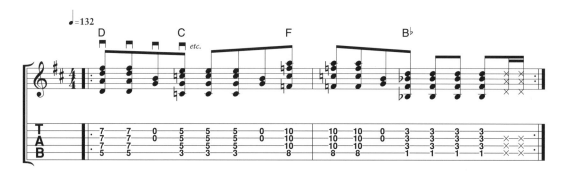

H

Words and music by:
Randy Fitzsimmons

From the album:
Veni Vidi Vicious (2000)

Highest chart placing (UK):
23 (2002)

Highest chart placing (US):
86 (2001)

Guitarists:
Nicolaus Arson (Treble)
Vigilante Carlstroem (Middle)

Set-up:
Fender Telecaster through a Fender Vibrolux
amplifier

How to get that sound:
Select the guitar's bridge pickup and leave the
controls fully open (10/10). At the amp, set the
gain to 7/10, high enough to clip, but not so high
that the single coil pickup sound is masked by a
wall of distortion. Tonally the sound is full of hi-
mid and presence, lacking low-mid and bass. One
further ingredient – don't be too shy with the
strumming, take a run up if you need to.

Fascinating fact:
According to the band, they were brought
together by a person named *Randy Fitzsimmons*.
Each member of the band received a letter telling
them when and where they were to meet, and so
it was that they found themselves at their first
rehearsal, each a stranger to the others. The band
claim that Mr Fitzsimmons writes their songs, both

the lyrics and the music, and he shows them how
to play the riffs. Guitarist Nicholaus Arson collects
the royalty payments and gives Fitzsimmons his
share in cash. There's no evidence that anyone
outside the band has even met him, apparently
Fitzsimmons "doesn't want to be famous", that is,
if he exists at all.
On only a slightly less perplexing note, the two
guitarists don't define themselves as lead and
rhythm, but rather as treble and middle. They list
their full instrumental line up as consisting of
vocals, treble, middle, bass and rhythm.

Most memorable lyric:
Do what I want cause I
Can and if I don't
Because I wanna
Be ignored by the stiff
And the bored
Because I'm gonna.

© 2002 Songs And Stories Publishing, Sweden
Warner/Chappell Artemis Music Ltd, London W6 8BS

H

Words and music by:
Billy Roberts

From the album:
Are You Experienced (1967)

Highest Chart Placing (UK):
6 (1967)

Guitarist:
Jimi Hendrix

Set-up:
Fender Stratocaster through a Marshall Stack

How to get that sound:
Yet another classic Fender Stratocaster/Marshall combination. The guitar is just below the point of distortion – set the Strat's toggle switch to the middle position and the gain to around 5/10. If you have a spring reverb unit in your amplifier set it to around 4/10 (they vary considerably), otherwise try using spring or plate reverb settings on digital effects.

Fascinating fact:
There's a lot of confusion over who wrote the song 'Hey Joe', with other songwriters claiming that the first person to copyright the song, Billy Roberts, 'borrowed' the melody and chord sequence and simply added new lyrics. The song even has a website dedicated to it, which lists over 600 groups who have recorded cover versions. You can visit the site at *www.heyjoe.org*.

Outrageous facts!
In 1968 Cynthia Albritton (a.k.a. *Cynthia Plaster Caster*) made a plaster cast of Jimi's penis. It is by far the largest in her collection, and she calls it the Penis De Milo. Cynthia's models include Noel Redding (Jimi Hendrix Experience), Eric Burden (The Animals), Pete Shelley (The Buzzcocks) and Jello Biafra (The Dead Kennedys). High on her 'To Do' list is Jarvis Cocker (Pulp).

To check out Jimi's whopper chopper, or even buy a limited edition casting (for a mere $1,500) visit *www.cynthiapcaster.org*.

Apparently, during Jimi's casting, the plaster broke into three sections on removal, so it's true – he really did break the mould.

Most memorable lyric:
Hey Joe
Where you goin' with that gun of your hand
Hey Joe, I said
Where you goin' with that gun in your hand
I'm goin' down to shoot my old lady
You know I caught her messin' 'round
With another man
Yeah, I'm goin' down to shoot my old lady
You know I caught her messin' 'round
With another man
Huh, and that ain't cool!

© 1962 Third Story Music Inc, USA
Carlin Music Corp, London NW1 8BD for PRS Territories only.

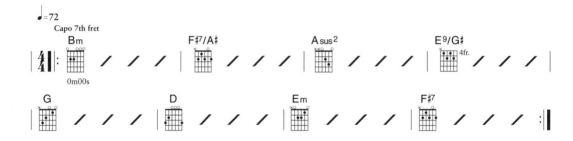

Words and music by:
Don Henley, Glenn Frey and Don Felder

From the album:
Hotel California (1976)

Highest chart placing (UK):
8 (1977)

Highest chart placing (US):
1 (1977)

Guitarists:
Don Felder
Joe Walsh
Glenn Frey
Randy Meisner

Set-up:
12-string guitar

How to get that sound:
The mandolin like sound of the 12-string guitar is partly a result of placing the capo at the 7th fret. Strings played in 'open' positions sound different, even with a capo, to those that are barred in the same position. Another critical variable to getting the right tone is where you pick the strings, move closer to the bridge for a sharper tone, and move towards the sound hole for a more rounded harp-like sound.

Fascinating fact:
The guitarist who probably did the most to popularise the 12-string guitar was Huddie 'Leadbelly' Ledbetter. He played with his guitar tuned two tones lower than normal for a deeper, more sonorous tone. (See 'Black Betty' – page 20)

Technical tips:
First and foremost, tune up properly – an out of tune 12-string guitar is what *Winston Smith* really should have confronted in Room 101. Unless you're a seasoned pro, just reach for the digital tuner right away.
Get the guitar roughly in tune and then put the capo on at the 7th and fine tune carefully.

Most memorable lyric:
Last thing I remember
I was running for the door
I had to find the passage back
To the place I was before
'Relax', said the night man
'We are programmed to receive
You can checkout any time you like
But you can never leave ...'

© 1976 Cass Country Music, Red Cloud Music and Fingers Music, USA
Warner/Chappell North America Ltd, London W6 8BS

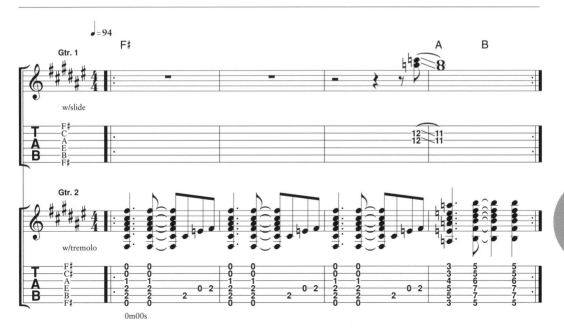

H

Words and music by:
Johnny Marr and Stephen Morrissey

From the album:
Hatful Of Hollow (1984)

Highest chart placing (UK):
24 (1985)

Guitarist:
Johnny Marr

Set-up:
Epiphone Casino through a Fender Twin Reverb

How to get that sound:
Set the gain to the maximum setting you can before distortion sets in. Use the bridge pickup on the guitar and leave all the tone controls fully open. Add about 5/10 reverb for a dark ambient feel, you won't hear this as an echo because there are no sudden stops in which the reverb will become obvious.
The original recording features several layered slide guitar parts played through an AMS harmoniser. Some parts were played on single strings, and the final part was played on the 2nd and 3rd strings together (notated here).

Fascinating fact:
The tremolo effect in the intro was created using the vibrato effect built into many Fender Twin amplifiers. Johnny and Smiths producer John Porter set up the studio sound room with a Fender Twin at each side facing into centre of the room. A pre-recorded rhythm guitar track was played through them while each man manually adjusted the vibrato control on two of the amplifiers. It took numerous takes to get the effect just right, something that could be achieved in very little time today with the use of a sampler.

Technical tips:
The slide guitar part (Gtr. 1 above) may well be the weirdest tuning you'll ever come across. The rhythm guitar parts of the song were recorded with the whole guitar tuned up by a tone, you'll notice if you do this that the song is a collection of standard open chords such as E, G, A and D. After recording the first few layered slide lines, Johnny tuned the second string down a semitone in order to play both notes together.

Most memorable lyric:
There's a club if you'd like to go
You could meet somebody who really loves you
So you go, and you stand on your own
And you leave on your own
And you go home
And you cry
And you want to die.

© 1985 Marr Songs Ltd and Bona Relations Ltd
Warner/Chappell Music Ltd, London W6 8BS and Copyright Control

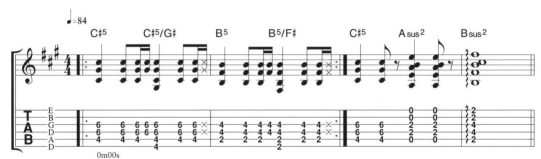

Tune guitar down a semitone to match key of original recording

Words and music by:
Chad Kroeger, Michael Kroeger, Ryan Peake and Ryan Vikedal

From the album:
Silver Side Up (2001)

Highest chart placing (UK):
4 (2002)

Highest chart placing (US):
4 (2002)

Guitarists:
Chad Kroeger & Ryan Peake

Set-up:
Paul Reed Smith (single cutaway) through Mesa Boogie Triple Rectifier

How to get that sound:
Set the guitar's pickup selector switch to the middle position and warm the sound using the amplifier's tone controls – aim to get an open acoustic sound. Add a moderate amount of chorus, enough to add a spatial dimension to the sound without the effect being too obvious. Use a light gauge pick to cut down on pick attack noise. This is one tune that will benefit greatly from the glassy tone of new strings.

Technical tips:
This is a good example of parallel harmony – the same chord is used throughout, with only one small change (the bass note additions in bars one and two). In bars one and two, changing between chords involves simply spanning an extra string with the barre.

Most memorable lyric:
Never made it as a wise man
I couldn't cut it as a poor man stealin'
Tired of livin' like a blind man
I'm sick inside without a sense of feelin'
And this is how you remind me
Of what I really am.

© 2001 Arm Your Dillo Publishing, Black Diesel Music Inc, Zero G Music Inc and Ladekiv Music Inc, USA
Warner/Chappell North America Ltd, London W6 8BS

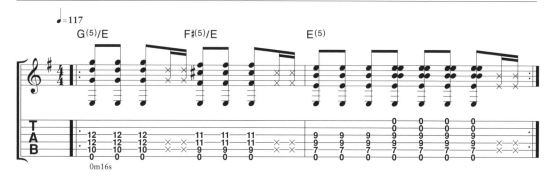

Words and music by:
James Osterberg, Scott Asheton, Ronald Asheton and David Alexander

From the album:
The Stooges (1969)

Guitarist:
Ron Asheton

Set-up:
Gibson Flying V through a Marshall Stack

How to get that sound:
Ron used a Dallas Arbiter Fuzz Face set for maximum fuzz. He then set the Marshall to 9/10, which was a compromise with producer John Cale (Velvet Underground) who thought 10/10 was unnecessary in the studio.

Fascinating fact:
Ths Stooges' final concert was captured on tape and released under the title *Metallic K.O.*. The previous night a biker gang called The Scorpions took exception to the band and began to pelt the stage with everything from eggs to beer bottles. Iggy Pop stopped the show and demanded that the thrower of one particularly effective missile step forward. The crowd parted revealing the biggest, meanest biker Iggy had ever seen. Charged with adrenalin and seemingly unperturbed by the biker's huge stature and full arm studded knuckle glove, Iggy launched rock'n'roll's least successful violent assault. He was K.O.'d with a single punch, but somehow, and in the finest showbiz tradition, he managed to rouse himself, return to the stage and complete the gig. The following day he invited the gang, on radio, to come to the next gig and "do your worst." The result is *'Metallic K.O.'*

Most memorable lyric:
Now I'm ready to close my eyes
And now I'm ready to close my mind
And now I'm ready to feel your hand
And lose my heart on the burning sands
And now I wanna be your dog
And now I wanna be your dog
Now I wanna be your dog
Well c'mon!

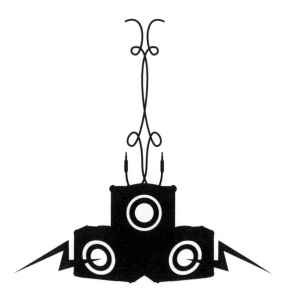

'The best way to kill your music is to sit down every day and work at it. You've got to sneak up on it and catch it when it's not looking.'
Iggy Pop

© 1969 (renewed) Warner-Tamerlane Publishing Corp and 8 Stooge Staffel Music, USA
Warner/Chappell North America Ltd, London W6 8BS

If It Makes You Happy

Sheryl Crow

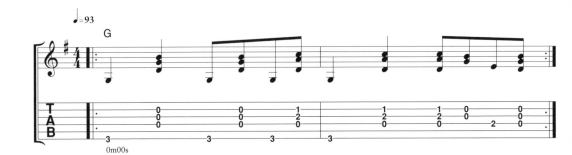

Words and music by:
Sheryl Crow and Jeff Trott

From the album:
Sheryl Crow (1996)

Highest chart placing (UK):
9 (1996)

Highest chart placing (US):
10 (1997)

Guitarist:
Jeff Trott

Set-up:
Gibson Les Paul Custom through a Vox AC30

How to get that sound:
This is a beautiful vintage tone! The key feature is the Vox AC30, an amp whose warm distortion digital engineers have been trying to master for years, with varying levels of success.
Firstly, select the bridge pickup on your guitar. If you have an AC30 it's just a question of turning the volume up to the required level and setting the tone – if not use an amplifier modelling effects unit. Failing both of those, use a *vintage overdrive* pedal in preference to a modern *super distortion* type pedal.
Bear in mind that amplifiers such as AC30s are very sensitive to the input signal, so adjusting the volume output from the guitar and the type of pickups you use can have a remarkable effect on the amplifier's overdrive characteristics. Jeff's 1973 Gibson Les Paul Custom has had its original pickups changed to Seymour Duncan '57s. These will have a far lower output than, for example, a DiMarzio X2N.

Most memorable lyric:
I belong a long way from here
Put on a poncho, played for mosquitoes
And drank 'til I was thirsty again
We went searching through thrift store jungles
Found Geronimo's rifle
Marilyn's shampoo
And Benny Goodman's corset and pen
Well, O.K. I made this up
I promised you I'd never give up
If it makes you happy
It can't be that bad
If it makes you happy
Then why the hell are you so sad?

© 1996 Old Crow Music and Trottsky Music, USA
Warner/Chappell North America Ltd, London W6 8BS and IQ Music Ltd, West Sussex RH16 3DT

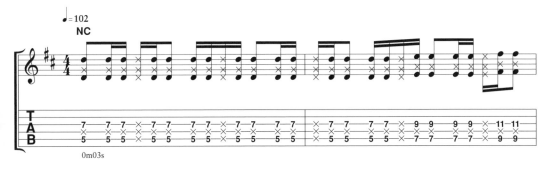

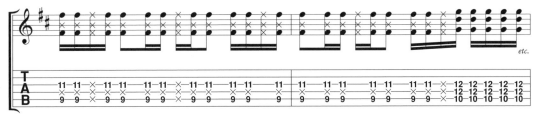

Words and music by:
Andy Bews, Colin Doran, Andy Gilmour, Larry Hibbitt and Paul Townsend

From the album:
Ideas Above Our Station (2002)

Guitarists:
Larry Hibbitt
Paul Townsend

Set-up:
1964 Gibson Les Paul Goldtop through a Marshall Stack

How to get that sound:
Select your bridge pickup and turn the amplifier gain up high (9/10). Perform only basic tonal shaping at the amplifier as the sound is not overly processed. Note that there is little if any reverb.

Technical tips:
When playing octaves like this you can damp the 'middle' string with your index finger. While the tip of the index finger needs to hold down the lower note of the octave, the damping can be executed by letting the underside of the fingertip lay flat across the string below. This necessitates a more relaxed 'flat' hand position, rather than being right up on your fingertips. Then again, maybe you're lazy and play like that all the time...

Most memorable lyric:
What could have happened to
Take what's become of this
Choices that he had made
Moulds to most of it
But to hide in the shade
Will keep the weather out
And to crawl into
The hole that hides you now.

© 2002 EMI Music Publishing Ltd, London WC2H 0QY

Words and music by:
Jimmy Page and Robert Plant

From the album:
Led Zeppelin III (1970)

Highest chart placing (UK):
16 (1970)

Guitarist:
Jimmy Page

Set-up:
1959 Les Paul Standard through a Marshall stack

How to get that sound:
Use the bridge guitar pickup and set the amplifier gain to a rather conservative 6/10. There are no other effects aside from the addition of a little reverb.

Fascinating fact:
While the *Led Zeppelin III* album was recorded at Headley Grange, in Hampshire, using The Rolling Stones mobile studio (see page 29 – 'Burn'), much of it was written by Page and Plant at a small cottage in Wales called Bron-Yr-Aur. In 1970 the house had no electricity, and this is said to be one reason for the more acoustic direction that the album took.
The album even includes an instrumental guitar piece titled Bron-Y-Aur, a slightly misspelt variation of the cottage's name.
Jimmy's taste in accommodation can also be seen in his purchase only a year later of *Boleskine House*, formerly owned by Aleister Crowley.

Technical tips:
Don't let the octave notes ring together in the opening two bars. This requires some deft picking. Notice the repeated two beat pattern, which should be picked *down down up down up up*.

Most memorable lyric:
We come from the land of the ice and snow
From the midnight sun
Where the hot springs blow
How soft your fields so green
Can whisper tales of gore
Of how we calmed the tides of war
We are your overlords
On we sweep with threshing oar
Our only goal will be the western shore.
So now you'd better stop
And rebuild all your ruins
For peace and trust can win the day
Despite of all your losing.

© 1970 Flames Of Albion Music Inc, USA
Warner/Chappell Music Ltd, London W6 8BS

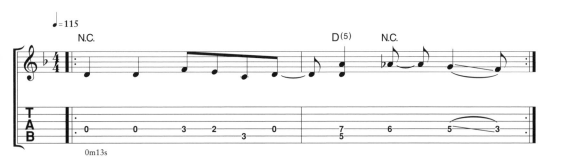

Words and music by:
Douglas Ingle

From the album:
In-A-Gadda-Da-Vida (1968)

Highest chart placing (US):
30 (1968)

Guitarist:
Erik Braunn

Set-up:
Mosrite guitar through Vox amplifiers

How to get that sound:
I've met guitarists who think the term *Fuzz Box* is just an old fashioned way of talking about distortion pedals. Obviously this isn't the case, and this song typifies the smoother side of what a fuzz box is capable of. Feed the guitar signal (bridge pickup) into something like a Dallas Arbiter Fuzz Face, set the unit to clip smoothly rather than the more aggressive fuzz we associate with T. Rex songs like '20th Century Boy'.

Fascinating fact:
An early classic chapter of rock mythology relates that Iron Butterfly vocalist and keyboardist, Doug Ingle, was so drunk during the writing of this song, that the rest of the band simply assumed it was called 'In-A-Gadda-Da-Vida', when in fact he had been singing "In The Garden Of Eden".
While a version of the song was re-released in 1995, cut down to around three minutes in length, the original album version is over 17 minutes long. This in itself was a short version as the band are said to have stretched it out to over an hour in live performance.

The album was a huge success, so much so that it is often credited as being the first platinum certified album by the RIAA, in truth this honour is actually held by The Eagles for the album *Their Greatest Hits 1971-1975.*

Most memorable lyric:
In-A-Gadda-Da-Vida, honey
Don't you know that I love you?
In-A-Gadda-Da-Vida, baby
Don't you know that I'll always be true?

© 1970 Iron Butterfly Inc, Ten East Music and Cotillion Music Inc, USA
Warner/Chappell Artemis Music Ltd, London W6 8BS

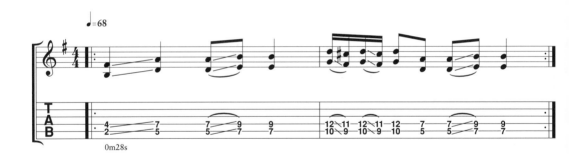

0m28s

I

Words and music by:
Terrence Butler, John Osbourne, Tony Iommi and William Ward

From the album:
Paranoid (1970)

Highest chart placing (US):
52 (1972)

Guitarist:
Tony Iommi

Set-up:
Gibson SG through a Laney stack

How to get that sound:
Choose the bridge pickup and run the signal through a Dallas Arbiter Fuzz Face set for a high (8/10) clip. The sound can be further lifted by placing a treble booster such as a Dallas Range Master before the Fuzz Face.

Fascinating fact:
On the day he was due to leave the factory at which he worked, Tony Iommi suffered an industrial accident that severed half of his middle finger and the tip from his ring finger. For a time his injuries did not allow him to hold down whole chord shapes, but eventually he made himself some 'thimbles' by melting and shaping the tops of Fairy Liquid bottles. Despite this he relied heavily on his index and little fingers, and in so doing 'invented' the power 5th chord which has driven rock music ever since.
By the way, don't go thinking that there was only one crazy loon in Black Sabbath, on his website *www.iommi.com* Tony relates the story of when he set fire to Bill Ward (the Sabbath drummer): "He went up like a Christmas tree [...] screamed and started rolling around on the floor. His clothes started burning and his socks melted – the nylon socks stuck to his leg. I wasn't able to help him because I couldn't stop laughing".

Most memorable lyric:
I am Iron Man!

'Of all the things I've lost, I miss my mind the most.'
Ozzy Osbourne

                                                        © 1970 Westminster Music Ltd, London SW10 0SZ

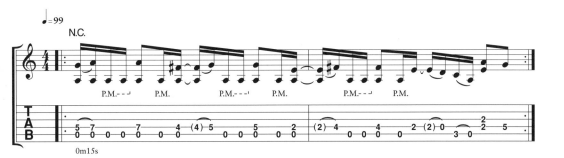

Words and music by:
Bobby Gillespie, Robert Young and Andrew Innes

From the album:
Give Out But Don't Give Up (1994)

Highest chart placing (UK):
29 (1994)

Guitarists:
Andrew Innes
Robert Young

Set-up:
Gibson Les Paul through a Marshall stack

How to get that sound:
This is a smooth, near saturated distortion with a pokey middly tone. Use the bridge pick on your guitar (at this point in the book you can begin to see why Eddie Van Halen simply removed all the other pickups). Set amp gain to around the 8/10 mark and leave the sound dry. Shape the sound with a graphic or parametric E.Q.

Technical tips:
The key to success in this riff is in careful control of muting. You need to be able to quickly alternate between muted notes and the hammer-ons or phrase endings. This is a key rhythm guitar skill and takes time and patience to master, however, once it finally clicks it should quickly become a nuance that you will add instinctively. Take on a few riffs like this to nail the technique and it will pay dividends.

Fascinating Fact:
At a Primal Scream gig in Glasgow, August 1997, 14 people were stabbed by an unidentified man with a hypodermic syringe.

Most memorable lyric:
Scratchin' like a tom cat
Got a monkey on my back
I'm gonna push and pull
And howl like wolf
And drive my Cadillac
I've got medication, honey
I've got wings to fly
I've got horse hoof tea
To buzz you like a bee
Gonna blind the evil eye
Push and pull with me
Funky jammin' free
Walk it like you talk it, honey
Strut your funky stuff
Come on...

© 1993 EMI Music Publishing Ltd, London WC2H 0QY and Complete Music Ltd, London SW6 3JH

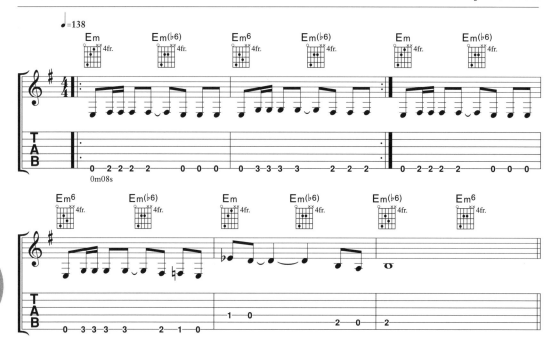

Music by:
Monty Norman

Highest chart placing (UK):
13 (1962) *John Barry Orchestra*
8 (1997) *Moby*

Guitarist:
Vic Flick (*John Barry Orchestra recording*)

Set-up:
Clifford Essex Paragon DeLuxe (w/DeArmond pickup) through a Vox 15w amplifier

How to get that sound:
This is something that has been eluding Vic ever since the soundtrack to *Dr No* was recorded in 1962. Of course, as he still owns all the equipment he can get quite close, but it's the finishing touches of microphone type and positioning, room acoustics and the final mastering stages that have made it impossible to catch that same moody atmosphere since.

Fascinating fact:
So how much has Vic made from playing in the *Bond* sessions? Legendary, timeless classics that have been screened and re-screened for over 40 years – factor in cinema, television and cable rights, vinyl, video, DVD and CD royalties and you could be forgiven for thinking that he must have been laughing all the way to the bank. The truth is that Vic was paid a total of £9 for his efforts as they were recorded at a time before such royalty payments were in effect.

© 1962 EMI United Partnership Ltd, USA
Worldwide print rights controlled by Warner Bros. Publications Inc/IMP Ltd

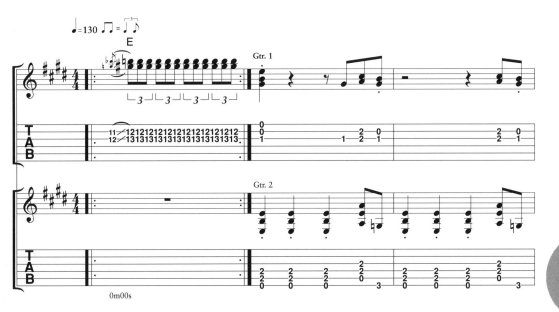

Words and music by:
David Bowie

From the album:
Aladdin Sane (1973)

Highest chart placing (UK):
2 (1972)

Highest chart placing (US):
71 (1972)

Guitarist:
Mick Ronson

Set-up:
1968 Gibson Les Paul Custom through a Marshall stack

How to get that sound:
Select the bridge pickup of your guitar and feed the signal through a fuzz box (Mick used a Vox Tone Bender fuzz pedal). Many guitar multi-effects units have a fuzz setting – if you don't have access to a proper fuzz effect opt for vintage overdrive rather than a more modern distortion sound. You need just a basic clip, so be conservative with the fuzz level. Shape the sound to emphasise the middle frequencies, it's possible that Mick used a wah-wah pedal set and left open at a pre-selected frequency to do this.

Most memorable lyric:
Sits like a man but smiles like a reptile
She love him
She love him but just for a short while
She'll scratch in the sand, won't let go his hand
He says he's a beautician
And sells you nutrition
And keeps all your dead hair
For making up underwear
Poor little Greenie.

© 1973 EMI Music Publishing Ltd, Moth Music and Tintoretto Music
EMI Music Publishing Ltd, London WC2H 0QY, Chrysalis Music Ltd, London W10 6SP and RZO Music Ltd, London W1M 5FF

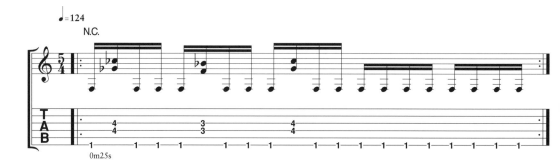

Words and music by:
Alain Jourgensen, Paul Barker, William Rieflin, Michael Balch and Gibson Haynes

From the album:
Psalm 69: The Way To Succeed And The Way To Suck Eggs (1992)

Guitarists:
Al Jourgensen
Mike Scaccia

How to get that sound:
This is a cut and dried case of turning everything way up and standing well back.

Fascinating fact:
Following the September 11th tragedy, anarchistic Ministry founder members Al Jourgensen and Paul Barker began sending e-mails loaded with words and phrases that were designed to draw the attention of ECHELON, the National Security Administration's (NSA) program that attempts to hunt down terrorists by monitoring e-mail and data transmissions for keywords such as 'nuclear' and 'bomb'. They soon became convinced that their houses were being bugged.

Technical tips:
The only way to play this riff is to stick to strict alternate picking throughout. The double stopped chord stabs can be played easily by using a 4th finger partial barre. Notice in the verse that the guitarists are playing in 5/4 while the drummer is playing in 4/4. Interestingly, by design or accident, the time signatures coincide exactly as the song moves into the chorus. The chorus is then either 4 bars of 5/4 or 5 bars of 4/4 depending on whether you're playing the guitar or the drums.

Most memorable lyric:
Soon I discovered
That this 'Rock' thing was true
Jerry Lee Lewis was the devil
Jesus was architect
Previous to his career as a prophet
All of a sudden
I found myself in love with the world
So there was only one thing I could do; was
Ding-a-ding dang my dang-a-long ling-long...

© 1992 Spurburn Music and Latino Buggerveil Music, USA
Warner/Chappell North America Ltd, London W6 8BS and Notting Hill Music (UK) Ltd, London W8 4AP

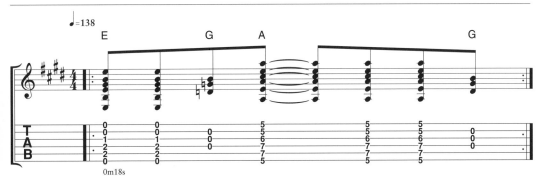

Words and music by:
Frederick Smith, Wayne Kambes, Dennis Tomich, Robert Derminer and Michael Davis

From the album:
Kick Out The Jams (1969)

Highest chart placing (US):
82 (1969)

Guitarists:
Fred Smith
Wayne Kramer

Set-up:
Mosrite Venture and Fender Stratocaster through Marshall stacks

How to get that sound:
MC5 would not have used Marshall Master Volume amplifiers, the distortion would be produced by driving the amps hard, *very hard*. For most of us (with neighbours) there's an easier method – dial in plenty of gain then moderate the output with the master volume on your amplifier. Make sure you use the bridge pickup and leave all volume/tone controls fully open on the guitar.

Fascinating fact:
The intro to this song features a choice word that rarely appears in print. On one occasion a vigilante club owner took it upon himself to invite the police to an MC5 gig that was happening at his premises. If the 'big taboo word' was mentioned, the police would move in and remove the band. Of course, that's exactly what happened, a struggle ensued with the band refusing to leave without being paid and a police officer was assaulted. Fred Smith

received a four day jail sentence while manager John Sinclair received six months, which was extended to ten years for a previous case involving possession of marijuana.

Most memorable lyric:
Kick out the jams motherf***ers!

'I'd set my amp up to sound the way I wanted, because I don't just play the guitar, I play the amp, too. That sound I got, it had an energy to it.' Wayne Kramer

© 1969 Warner-Tamerlane Publishing Corp, USA
Warner/Chappell North America Ltd, London W6 8BS

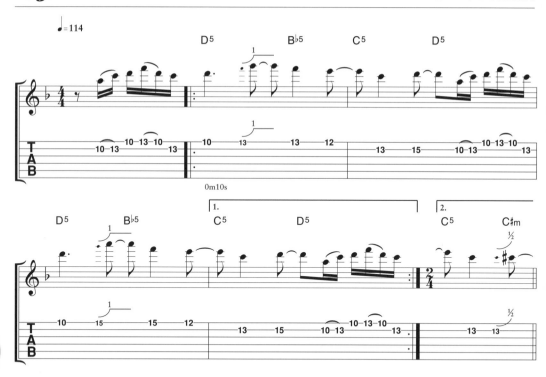

Words and music by:
Jim Gordon and Eric Clapton

From the album:
Layla And Other Assorted Love Songs (1970)

Highest chart placing (UK):
7 (1972)
4 (1982) (re-issue)

Highest chart placing (US):
10 (1972)

Guitarist:
Eric Clapton

Set-up:
Fender Stratocaster through Fender Tweed Champ and Pignose amplifiers

How to get that sound:
In many ways the guitar sound used for this riff is the least interesting of all of the layered guitars on the track. A Stratocaster bridge pickup will give you the most authentic timbre – add enough gain to create a solid crunch.

Fascinating fact:
This riff, although played by Eric, is rumoured to have been written by guitarist Duane Allman who also appears on the album. Furthermore, the piano outro was written by the drummer Jim Gordon. The words, however, were penned by Eric, who had been given a copy of the book *The Story of Layla and Majnun* by 12th century Azerbaijani poet Nizami. The story's tale of forbidden love inspired him to write 'Layla' – a private (although publicly released!) message to George Harrison's wife, Patti Boyd. Eric had become besotted with Patti and would later marry her. Just in case you're feeling sorry for George, or angry with Eric, George played at the wedding, so either it was alright by him or he seriously needed the work.

© 1976 Eric Clapton and Throat Music Ltd
Warner/Chappell Music Ltd, London W6 8BS

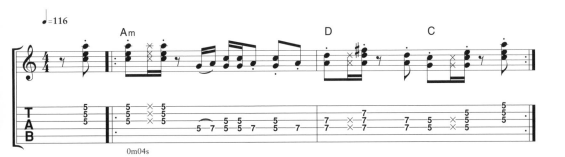

Words and music by:
Bernard Edwards and Nile Rodgers

From the album:
C'est Chic (1978)

Highest chart placing (UK):
7 (1978)

Highest chart placing (US):
1 (1978)

Guitarist:
Nile Rodgers

Set-up:
Tokai Stratocaster

How to get that sound:
See page 43 – 'Good Times'

Fascinating fact:
On New Year's Eve, 1977, Chic guitarist Nile Rodgers and bassist Bernard Edwards arrived at the doors of *Studio 54*, the legendary New York club. They were there to see Grace Jones who was performing that night, and wanted Nile and Bernard to appear on her next album. For some reason nobody bothered to pass this message on the doormen, who resolutely refused to allow the pair in. No doubt the doormen simply assumed they were a couple of chancers sporting sharp suits with huge collars in an attempt to look like they were in Chic, but all protestations fell on deaf ears, and the guys returned to the studio. In a creative outpour fuelled by the incident, they wrote, in about 25 minutes flat, a catchy little number that started "AhhHHHH F*** Off!". It

dawned on the men that they had a hit on their hands, and inevitably the original hook line was watered down to reflect a dance that they had seen called '*the freak*'.
Many people thought that Chic were deluded in trying to launch another dance craze, but they believed it could be as big as '*the twist*'. After a slack start, record sales began to rocket, eventually topping five million in the US, while in Canada it became the biggest selling single of all time.

Most memorable lyric:
All that pressure got you down
Has your head spinning all around
Feel the rhythm, check the ride
Come on along and have a real good time
Like the days of stomping at the Savoy
Now we freak, oh what a joy
Just come on down, to Fifty Four
Find a spot out on the floor.

Aaahh freak out!
Le freak, c'est chic
Freak out!

Now freak!

[This is the cue for everyone on the dance floor to do a crazy 70s dance involving more pelvic thrusting than the 'Time Warp']

I said freak!

[... more encouragement – this time clap along too]

Now freak!

[... really go to town this time!]

© 1978 Bernard's Other Music and Sony/ATV Songs LLC, USA
Warner/Chappell Music Ltd, London W6 8BS and Sony/ATV Music Publishing, London W1V 2LP

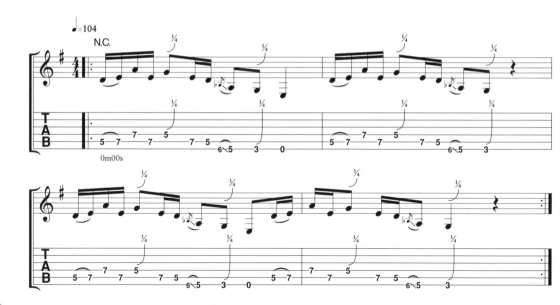

Words and music by:
Don Henley, Glenn Frey and Joe Walsh

From the album:
Hotel California (1976)

Highest chart placing (US):
11 (1977)

Guitarist:
Joe Walsh

Set-up:
Gibson Les Paul through a Fender Twin amplifier

Fascinating fact:
The title of this tune comes from an incident when Glenn Frey was sitting in the passenger seat of a car being driven by a drug dealer who went under the name of *'The Count'*. They were late for a poker game with the rest of The Eagles, and The Count put his foot to the floor and moved to the outer lane. Glenn told The Count that he was driving too fast, to which The Count replied "Hey, man, it's life in the fast lane."

How to get that sound:
Use the bridge guitar pickup through an amp set for mild crunch (gain 6/10).

Most memorable lyric:
Eager for action
And hot for the game
The coming attraction
The drop of a name
They knew all the right people
They took all the right pills
They threw outrageous parties
They paid heavenly bills
There were lines on the mirror
Lines on her face
She pretended not to notice
She was caught up in the race.

© 1978 Cass Country Music, Red Cloud Music and Wow And Flutter Music, USA
Warner/Chappell North America Ltd, London W6 8BS and Warner/Chappell Music Ltd, London W6 8BS

Words and music by:
Paul McCartney and Linda McCartney

From the film:
Live And Let Die (1973)

Highest chart placing (UK):
9 (1973)

Highest chart placing (US):
2 (1973)

Guitarist:
Henry McCullough

How to get that sound:
Use the bridge guitar pickup and leave all the controls fully open. Set the amplifier gain to about 8/10 for a good distorted tone, but don't allow the sound to venture into saturation. Use a wah pedal set at a fixed point (it's up to you to experiment here) to boost the middle and get that nasal guitar tone.

Fascinating fact:
In 1973 'Live And Let Die' was nominated as *Best Original Song* in the Academy Awards. Paul was nominated in the same category again in 2002 for 'Vanilla Sky'. While he hasn't acheived the ultimate accolade and taken home the 'song gong' he must have one of the little statuettes somewhere as in 1971 The Beatles won *Best Original Score* for 'Let It Be'.
'Live And Let Die' also allowed Paul to work again with producer George Martin. Paul was invited originally to be the writer of the song only, as the producers preferred the title song to feature a female vocalist, however Paul simply stated that if they wanted a McCartney song, it would have to be performed by his group, Wings.

Technical tips:
This is very easy to play, and as such it's suitable for any novices who may be struggling with some of the harder pieces in this book. It's in the dorian mode, which is the same as the natural minor scale but with the sixth note of the scale played a semitone higher. This produces a brighter and more modern feel, and is often used in rock music.

Most memorable lyric:
When you were young
And your heart was an open book
You used to say live and let live
You know you did
You know you did
You know you did
But if this ever-changing
World in which we live in
Makes you give in and cry
Say 'Live and Let Die'.

L

© 1973 MPL Communications Inc, EMI Catalogue Partnership, EMI Unart Catalog Inc and EMI United Partnership Ltd, USA.
Worldwide print rights controlled by Warner Bros. Publications Inc/IMP Ltd and MPL Communications Ltd, London W1D 3BQ

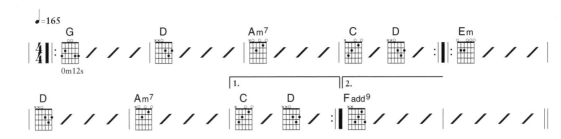

Words and music by:
Noel Gallagher

From the album:
Definitely Maybe (1994)

Highest chart placing (UK):
10 (1994)

Guitarist:
Noel Gallagher

Set-up:
Epiphone Riviera through a Vox AC30

How to get that sound:
For best results use a semi-acoustic guitar with humbucking pickups, use the bridge pickup and leave volume and tone controls wide open. Set the gain to the point at which a normal strum gives you only a hint of crunch but a loud strum is obviously overdriving. Add some phaser (don't go overboard) and compression (preferably not before the preamp – use an effects loop). Finish the sound with some reverb and tone contouring at the amp – make sure there's some 'jangle' in the verse and 'bite' in the chorus.

Fascinating fact:
Noel used to be a roadie for Manchester band Inspiral Carpets, having initially been turned down as a vocalist, but gave it up to join Oasis, the group that had been set up by his brother Liam. It was Noel's songwriting ability and music industry knowledge gleaned from his time with The Inspiral Carpets that convinced Liam that Noel should be allowed to join the band, but in the end it was a stroke of sheer luck rather than business accumen

that gave them their break.
Oasis were discovered in *King Tut's Wah Wah Hut*, a Glasgow venue famous for being the venue in which Oasis were discovered, and which takes its name from a venue in New York called *King Tut's Wah Wah Hut*. Creation Records boss Alan McGee happened upon the gig after missing his train and offered the band a record deal on the spot.

Most memorable lyric:
Maybe I just want to fly
Want to live I don't want to die
Maybe I just want to breathe
Maybe I just don't believe
Maybe you're the same as me
We see things they'll never see
You and I are gonna live forever.

© 1994 Oasis Music
Sony/ATV Music Publishing, London W1V 2LP

Words and music by:
Desmond Child, Jon Bon Jovi and Richie Sambora

From the album:
Slippery When Wet (1986)

Highest chart placing (UK):
4 (1986)

Highest chart placing (US):
1 (1987)

Guitarist:
Richie Sambora

Set-up:
Jackson or Kramer Superstrat through a Heil TalkBox

How to get that sound:
Select the bridge humbucker and leave all the guitar controls at 10/10. Set the amp up with the gain at 9/10, the distortion should be fairly saturated. Run the signal through a talk box (see *Fascinating Fact*).

Fascinating fact:
The talkbox is an effects pedal like no other. It allows guitarists to 'vocalise' their guitar sound by using their mouth as a resonator (in much the same way as you can with a jew's harp). To connect it up, you take the speaker output from your amplifier (yes... the speaker output!) and run it through the input on the talkbox. This signal powers a small metal driver unit which is connected to a plastic tube. With me so far? So, in effect, we have an amplifier that's forcing all of its sound through a plastic tube instead of a 4x12 cab.

The tube is then run up a microphone stand and the end overshoots the microphone by a couple of inches. The player can then put his mouth over the tube and create wild and wacky effects by miming the chorus of Kate Bush's 'Wow' (stopping short of 'Unbelievable'). When the TalkBox is activated the speaker cabinet is bypassed and the effected sound is picked up by the mic and fed to the P.A. system or back through the amp.
There are a couple of cautionary notes that should be observed. Firstly, using a high powered amplifier with the TalkBox can make you gag, loosen your teeth or blow your amplifier up – make sure your oesophagus, molars and speaker cab can take the strain, eat a light breakfast and go to bed early the night before. Secondly, guitarists have been electrocuted by trying to modify the speaker output of combo amps themselves – have an electrician carry out the work for you if you want to avoid that 'crimped hair' look for the rest of your life.

Most memorable lyric:
Wohhhhh
We're half-way there
Wohhhhh
Livin' on a prayer
Take my hand and we'll make it – I swear
Wohhhhh
Livin' on a prayer.

© 1985 EMI April Music Inc, Desmobile Music Co Inc, Bon Jovi Publishing and 810 Publishing Inc, USA
EMI Songs Ltd, London WC2H 0QY and Universal Music Publishing Ltd, London W6 8JA

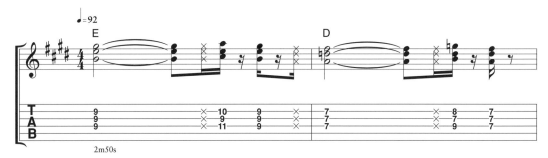

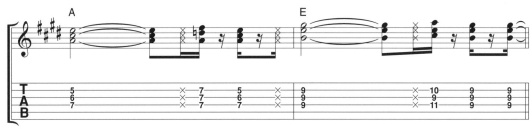

Words and music by:
Bobby Gillespie, Robert Young and Andrew Innes

From the album:
Screamadelica (1991)

Highest chart placing (UK):
15 (1990)

Guitarists:
Andrew Innes
Robert Young

Set-up:
Gibson Les Paul through a Marshall stack

How to get that sound:
The guitar on this track is heavily E.Q.'d, probably as a result of all the sampling and remixing by DJ Andy Weatherall who shaped the track into a club classic from original elements of an earlier Primal Scream track, 'I'm Losing More Than I'll Ever Have'.

Use a bridge mounted humbucker and leave the guitar controls fully open. Shape the signal at the amp or with a graphic or parametric equaliser to remove some of the middle frequencies. Set the amplifier for moderate distortion with gain of around 7/10. The result should sound slightly artificial.

Technical tips:
You can avoid striking unwanted strings when playing partial chords like these by being a little lazy with your hand position. Instead of getting right up onto your fingertips to allow open strings to ring out, allow the tips and undersides of your fingers to lay across or press onto the strings you don't want to sound. With a little practice you can be very selective about which strings are allowed to sound.

Most memorable lyric:
We wanna be free
We wanna be free to do what we wanna do
And we wanna get loaded
And we want to have a good time
And that's what we're gonna do
We're gonna have a good time
We're gonna have a party!

[A sample of the actor Peter Fonda – from the film *Wild Angels* (1966)]

© 1990 EMI Music Publishing Ltd, London WC2H 0QY and Complete Music Ltd, London SW6 3JH

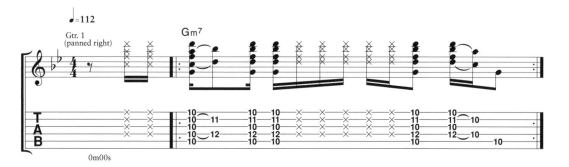

Words and music by:
Tom Johnston

From the album:
The Captain & Me (1973)

Highest chart placing (UK):
7 (1993) *Doobie Brothers*

Highest chart placing (US):
8 (1973)

Guitarists:
Tom Johnston
Patrick Simmons

Set-up:
Fender Stratocaster and a steel string acoustic guitar

How to get that sound:
There are several layers of acoustic and electric guitars on this track. The intro features steel string acoustic doubled by a Stratocaster. You can replicate the electric sound fairly easily with any guitar fitted with single coil pickups – experiment with pickup selection as there is such a variety of pickup and wiring configuration on these instruments.

Drive the amplifier so that the guitar is only just distorting. You could call this a 'gainy clean' or 'clean distortion' sound: if you add too much gain you'll lose the detail of the chord tones, add too little and it will sound like a Nile Rodgers disco number. Actual amp selection is less critical than the pickup/gain settings, but if you have a choice of amps or amp modelling effects, start with a 'classic' rather than hi-gain amplifier.

Fascinating fact:
The term 'Doobie' is commonly used to mean a marijuana cigarette or 'joint'. As there are no siblings in the Doobie Brothers, we can only assume the term indicates the band had a fondness for smoking dope. If you really want to draw the attention of the authorities you could scarcely find a better name for your band, as is proved by Tom Johnston's arrest in 1973 on possession charges. However, the name can only be seen as a sensible move in light of their former name, *Pud*.

Curious covers:
Bananarama reached number 30 in the UK charts with this song – it featured on their album *Pop Life* (1991).

Most memorable lyric:
The Illinois Central
And the Southern Central freight
Gotta keep on pushin' mama
'Cause you know they're runnin' late
Without love
Where would you be now (now, now, now)
Without love?

© 1973 Warner-Tamerlane Publishing Corp, USA
Warner/Chappell North America Ltd, London W6 8BS

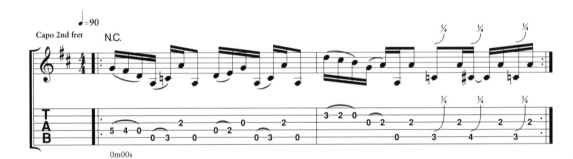

Words and music by:
John Squire

From the album:
Do It Yourself (1997)

Highest chart placing (UK):
3 (1997)

Guitarist:
John Squire

Set-up:
Gibson Les Paul through a Marshall stack

How to get that sound:
This is a rich full-bodied humbucker tone fed straight into a tube amp without any other effects. Select the bridge position pickup and leave all the guitar controls fully open. Set the amplifier gain to around 8/10 and ensure that the bass tone control produces a good fat timbre without making the sound too bottom heavy.

Technical tips:
The first problem you'll come across is getting the guitar in tune with a capo on. Do a quick rough tune up and then add the capo, once fitted you should spend a little longer fine tuning.
This riff clearly shows the influence of Jimmy Page on John's playing. It's essential to the sound and flow of the riff to observe all hammer-on and pull-off combinations. Allow the A octave notes to ring together throughout, along with the open G in the third beat in bar one, but be careful not to let any of the notes on the 4th string continue into another phrase – this will keep the riff firmly centred around A pentatonic.

Most memorable lyric:
Strap-on Sally chased us down the alley
We feared for our behinds
Oasis was a shop with shoes so hot
They were sure to blow your mind
Running so fast I can taste the past
Oh take me home.

© 1997 PolyGram Music Publishing Ltd
Universal Music Publishing Ltd, London W6 8JA

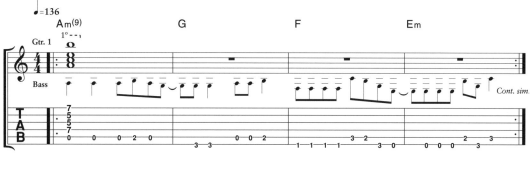

Words and music by:
Robert Smith, Simon Gallup, Boris Williams, Roger O'Donnell, Porl Thomson and Laurence Tolhurst

From the album:
Disintegration (1989)

Highest chart placing (UK):
18 (1989)

Highest chart placing (US):
2 (1989)

Guitarist:
Robert Smith

Set-up:
Fender Jazzmaster through a Roland Jazz Chorus

Fascinating fact:
When Robert turned up to record The Cure's first album, he took with him a *Top 20* guitar, bought from Woolworths for about £20. Producer Chris Parry told Robert that he couldn't use the guitar, so Robert went out and bought a Fender Jazzmaster because he 'liked the shape'.
Chris's initial relief turned once again to frustration after Robert immediately replaced the Jazzmaster pickups with those from his old Woolies guitar.

Most memorable lyric:
Whenever I'm alone with you
You make me feel like I am young again
Whenever I'm alone with you
You make me feel like I am fun again.

'When I was young I always dreamed of having a group that was adored by few and ignored by the rest of the world, like Nick Drake. Fortunately, when we became famous, I had no time to reflect upon anything anymore.'
Robert Smith

© 1987 Fiction Songs Ltd, London W1D 3JB

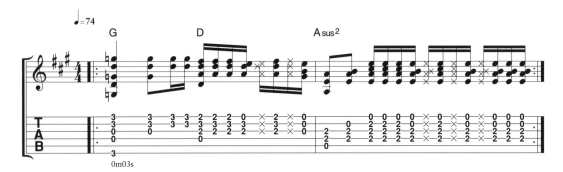

Words and music by:
Richard Ashcroft

From the album:
Urban Hymns (1997)

Highest chart placing (UK):
7 (1997)

Guitarists:
Richard Ashcroft
Simon Tong
Nick McCabe

Set-up:
Steel string acoustic guitar

How to get that sound:
Using a light gauge plectrum will make it easy to maintain a consistent attack on the strings. Because acoustic guitars often have a higher action than electrics, they are more susceptible to intonation errors, particularly around the first few frets where increased tension caused by a larger step at the nut can drag the notes out of tune.

If you're only going to be playing open chords you can often get better results by tuning the actual chords in the song rather than by using a tuner on open strings or harmonics. If you can tune well by ear you probably already know this trick, but it can be done easily with a chromatic tuner.

Hold down the chord – in this case let's choose the D chord – and then tune each note with reference to the chromatic tuner. When you're done, double check another chord from the song, maybe the G chord. This is useful in the studio, but less so on stage where audience 'booing' can be distracting.

The other riff:
In case you were disappointed that this isn't the little six note electric guitar hook, here's how it's played - hammer on the first, then second, then third open strings to the second fret.

Most memorable lyric:
Happiness
Something in my own place
I'm stood here naked
Smiling, I feel no disgrace
With who I am
Happiness
Coming and going
I watch you look at me
Watch my fever growing
I know just who I am.

© 1996 EMI Virgin Music Ltd, London WC2H 0QY

Rhythm:

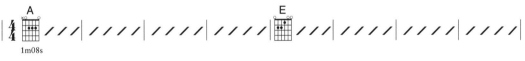

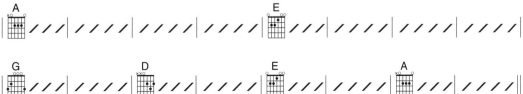

Words and music by:
David Bowie and James Osterberg

From the album:
Lust For Life (1977)

Highest chart placing (UK):
26 (1996)

Guitarists:
Carlos Alomar
Ricky Gardiner

Fascinating fact:
David Bowie and Iggy Pop collaborations go back some years before the release of 'Lust For Life'. Bowie appeared on Iggy's first solo release, *Idiot*, in 1973. One of the songs from *Idiot* was later released by Bowie, with Stevie Ray Vaughan and Nile Rodgers (see page 43 'Good Times' and page 63 'Le Freak') taking guitar duties. The song went to No. 2 in the UK charts and No. 10 in the US charts. By comparison Iggy's best chart success has been with 'Candy' in the US (No. 28) and 'Real Wild Child' in the UK (No. 10).
It should come as no surprise that Iggy was one of a number of influences on Bowie's *Ziggy Stardust*.

How to get that sound:
There are a lot of different guitar sounds in this track, but the most distinctive is one of the Fender Stratocaster's 'out of phase' sounds. This is produced by setting the pickup selector switch to the second position, and produces a punchy 'honk' tone. Before Stratocasters had five-position switches, players would get this sound by precariously balancing a three-position switch at a halfway point between the notches.

Most memorable lyric:
I'm worth a million in prizes
With my torture film
Drive a GTO
Wear a uniform
All on a government loan.

© 1977 EMI Music Publishing Ltd, Tintoretto Music and James Osterberg Music, USA
EMI Music Publishing Ltd, London WC2H 0QY, EMI Virgin Music Ltd, London WC2H 0QY and RZO Music Ltd, London W1M 5FF

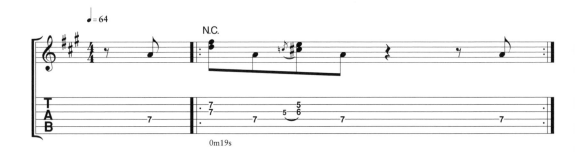

Words and music by:
Ellas McDaniels, Melvin London and McKinley Morganfield

Guitarist:
Muddy Waters

Set-up:
Fender Telecaster through a Fender Super Reverb

How to get that sound:
The Telecaster tone is very distinctive, particularly when the signal isn't driven hard into overdrive. If you don't own a Tele, use a Stratocaster or similar guitar with single coil pickups.
Muddy's favoured Fender Blackface Super Reverb doesn't sound as harsh as the natural sound you'll find coming from more recently designed amplifiers where the characteristics are optimised for distorted timbres – they have a more rounded, punchy bottom end that would be intrusive in a high gain situation. If you're fortunate enough to own effects equipment incorporating 'amp modelling' then choose the Blackface or Tweed models as your starting point. Add enough gain to add an edge without straying into outright overdrive, and make sure the signature of the single coil pickups is retained.
Avoid using a really crisp modern reverb, instead you should opt for a spring or plate reverb where available.

Fascinating fact:
While Muddy's influence can be seen everywhere from the work of Jimi Hendrix to The Rolling Stones, he never achieved the commercial success of those that he inspired. Keith Richards tells of a time when he visited Chess Studios in '64, the studio owner and sound engineer were waiting to meet them, and in the corner was a man in white overalls painting the ceiling. Keith was shocked when he realised it was the man he had idolised since his childhood, Muddy Waters, reduced to the position of studio painter and decorator in the face of dwindling record sales. Fortunately his popularity and rightful reputation as a founding father of both rock and blues were slowly restored, culminating in some seminal work with guitarist Johnny Winter.

Most memorable lyric:
I'm a man
I'm a full grown man
I'm a man
I'm a rollin' stone
I'm a man
I'm a hoochie coochie man.

© 1965 Arc Music Corp and Watertoons Music, USA
Tristan Music Ltd, London SW6 5SH and Bug Music Ltd, London W14 0LJ

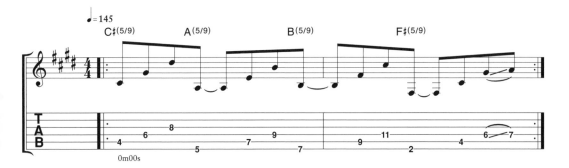

Words and music by:
Gordon Sumner

From the album:
Reggatta De Blanc (1979)

Highest chart placing (UK):
1 (1979)

Highest chart placing (US):
74 (1979)

Guitarist:
Andy Summers

Set-up:
Custom Fender Telecaster through a Fender Twin

How to get that sound:
The key effects to use in 'Message In A Bottle' are a flanger, set with a fairly slow sweep, and a compressor, which will tighten and fatten the sound. Drive the amp hard enough to add some edge, but without straying into distortion.
Andy's Telecaster has a Gibson humbucker fitted in the neck position, enabling him to get a fatter, rockier tone than a standard Tele with single coil pickups only.
Before the digital rack revolution, Andy favoured pedals by MXR, such as the Phase 90, Distortion Plus and Dynacomp compressor, along with those made by Electro-Harmonix such as the Electric Mistress flanger. He would use two Echoplex units to create complex multi-tap delay effects.
Many of these marques are part of a thriving market in used 'vintage' effects at online markets such as eBay, where they can command higher prices than brand new re-issued models by the original makers.

Fascinating fact:
In 1973, when Andy returned to the UK from a five year stint in Los Angeles, he was almost penniless and didn't even own an amplifier. He badly needed work and was pointed in the direction of Neil Sedaka by his friend Robert Fripp. Sedaka hired him and lent him the money for an amplifier without even hearing him play. Of course, this was at a time when guitarists generally weren't considered a nuisance.

Most memorable lyric:
Walked out this morning
I don't believe what I saw
A hundred billion bottles
Washed up on the shore
Seems I'm not alone at being alone
A hundred billion castaways
All looking for a home.

© 1979 Magnetic Publishing Ltd, London W1D 3JB

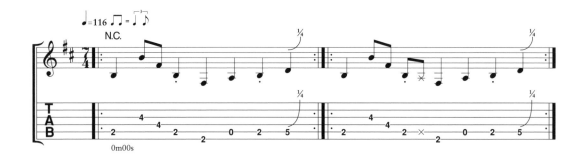

Words and music by:
George Roger Waters

From the album:
Dark Side Of The Moon (1973)

Highest chart placing (US):
13 (1973)

Guitarist:
David Gilmour

Set-up:
Fender Stratocaster through Hiwatt 100-watt head and WEM 4x12

How to get that sound:
This is simply a clean Stratocaster tone doubled by the bass guitar.

Fascinating fact:
The intro to 'Money' features sound effects created by multiple tape loops. Sections of tape were recorded, then cut and spliced into loops that were carefully measured to keep them in time. Cash register sounds from a sound effects record were mixed with home grown recordings of tearing paper and coins thrown into a bowl to create the final montage.
Such tape experimentation continued throughout Pink Floyd's career and culminated in the finest, most terrifying backwards 'satanic message' of them all, found on the track 'Empty Spaces' from *The Wall*. Devotees who risked their styli by spinning the records backward were treated to "Congratulations, You have just discovered the secret message. Please send your answer to Old Pink, care of the funny farm, Chalfont."

Technical tips:
If you haven't played in odd meter time signatures such as 7/4 it may help to think of it as being a bar of 4/4 followed by a bar of 3/4. Sometimes musicians will write such time signatures as 7/4 (4/4 + 3/4) to show where emphasis occurs within the bar. Another popular variation would be 7/8 (3/8 + 2/8 + 2/8) which would be counted 1-2-3 1-2 1-2 instead of 1-2-3-4-5-6-7.

Most memorable lyric:
Money, get back
I'm all right jack
Keep your hands off of my stack
Money, it's a hit
Don't give me that do-goody-good bulls***
I'm in the high-fidelity first class travelling set
And I think I need a Lear jet.

© 1973 Roger Waters Music Overseas Ltd
Warner/Chappell Artemis Music Ltd, London W6 8BS

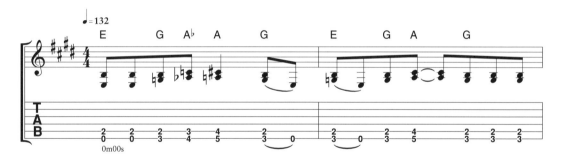

Words and music by:
Berry Gordy and Janie Bradford

From the album:
With The Beatles (1963)

Guitarists:
George Harrison
John Lennon

Set-up:
George:
Gretsch 6122 'Country Gentleman'

John:
Rickenbacker 325 1958

Amplification:
Vox AC30

How to get that sound:
The two guitars featured on this track have very individual tones that are very difficult to reproduce without very similar instruments. There are plenty of very well made modern replicas but they tend to be very expensive. Cheaper modern copies may well have better pickups and electronics that, on the one hand, improve the signal to noise ratio, but on the other fail to provide the charm and charisma of their older counterparts. If you don't have, or can't afford, either, semi-acoustics will provide the woody tone and shorter sustain of the older instruments, and you could try fitting flat wound strings to get away from the 'zing' of modern nickel strings.
Unless you own the real thing, vintage amplifier sounds are best emulated by modern modelling technology. The AC30 is considered a classic, and is included in nearly all amp modelling effects.

Fascinating fact:
This song was performed at The Beatles' Decca Records audition. In what is generally agreed to be the biggest A&R blunder of all time, Decca rejected the Fab Four, who went on to be snapped up by Parlophone.

Technical tips:
This is a good riff for novice players, use your first finger to play the second fret note in the first chord. Don't try to be clever with the rest, just follow the chords up with your first and second fingers.

Most memorable lyric:
The best things in life are free
But you can keep it for the birds and bees
Now gimme money (that's what I want)
That's what I want (that's what I want)
That's what I want, yeah, yeah, yeah
That's what I want.

© 1960 Jobete Music Co Inc and Stone Agate Music, USA
Jobete Music (UK) Ltd, London WC2H 0QY

77

Intro Riff:

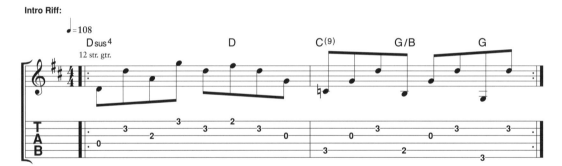

Chorus Riff:

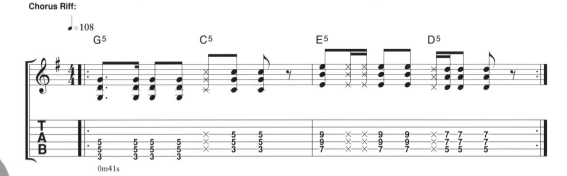

0m41s

Words and music by:
Tom Scholz

From the album:
Boston (1976)

Highest chart placing (UK):
22 (1977)

Highest chart placing (US):
5 (1976)

Guitarist:
Tom Scholz

Set-up:
12-string Guitar
1968 Gibson Les Paul Goldtop through a Marshall stack

How to get that sound:
Tom used a home made power soak, similar to the Variac used by Eddie Van Halen, to enhance the saturation of the amp's overdrive. His guitar's original P90 pickups were replaced with DiMarzio Super Distortion types. The middle frequencies were boosted by means of a fixed wah (putting a wah-wah pedal in the middle position and simply leaving it there).

The guitar sound was enormously influential, and Tom created a host of guitar effects units based around it which sold under the *Rockman* name. This is probably the easiest way to get his signature guitar sound. Many modelling effects units also include the 'More Than A Feeling' sound as a demo preset, although interestingly Tom has no time for digital equipment.

Fascinating fact:
The whole of *Boston* was recorded in Tom's basement. Tom played every instrument on the album apart from the drums, and had to form a scratch band at short notice to convince the record companies it could be reproduced live. When signed, the bogus band booked studio time in Los Angeles and pretended to record the album while Tom finished it off in his basement.

The record has sold over 20 million copies to date and was in the *Billboard* chart for 132 weeks.

Most memorable lyric:
I woke up this morning and the sun was gone
Turned on some music to start my day
I lost myself in a familiar song
I closed my eyes and I slipped away ...

© 1975 Pure Songs, USA
Warner/Chappell Music Ltd, London W6 8BS

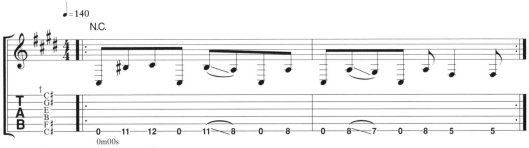

† Standard tuning down a tone and a half

Words and music by:
Camillo Moreno, Chi Cheng, Stephen Carpenter and Abe Cunningham

From the album:
Around The Fur (1997)

Highest chart placing (UK):
29 (1998)

Guitarist:
Stephen Carpenter

Set-up:
ESP Custom Horizon through Marshall JMP-1 pre-amp, EL34 100/100 power-amp and Marshall cabinet.

How to get that sound:
This track is driven by a high output guitar running hot humbuckers through a valve amp set to hi-gain (9/10 or even 10/10). Much of the depth is down to the tuning, but you should aim to compensate for the effect this tuning has on your guitar's sound with the amplifier tone controls.

Fascinating fact:
Many guitarists prefer the sound that is produced by tuning the guitar lower than the standard 'E tuning', but it's nothing new. Blues guitarist Leadbelly (1885-1949) would often tune lower to improve his tone.
Rock players have long tuned down a semitone either by design or because they haven't checked with a tuning device before recording.
Since the 80s metal bands have tuned to E♭ (a semitone lower) because it can have a stabilising effect on tuning when using a 'whammy' tremolo system. Baritone guitars, specially designed for lower tunings, are becoming popular instruments. A leading exponent is Jazz guitarist Pat Metheny who favours the acoustic baritone guitar, and Stephen himself has been experimenting with an electric baritone guitar.

Technical tips:
If your guitar is fitted with a whammy bar, engage its locking mechanism before tuning down this far. If you plan on keeping your guitar in this tuning you may well have to set it up especially to cope with the lower tension.

Most memorable lyric:
SHOVE IT
SHOVE IT
SHOVE IT
SHOVE IT
SHOVE IT
SHOVE IT
SHOVE IT
SHOVE IT

© 1997 My Rib It's Broke Music and Maverick Music Co, USA
Warner/Chappell North America Ltd, London W6 8BS

Words and music by:
Douglas Fieger and Berton Averre

From the album:
Get The Knack (1979)

Highest chart placing (UK):
6 (1979)

Highest chart placing (US):
1 (1979)

Guitarist:
Berton Averre

Set-up:
Gibson Les Paul through a Fender Vibro King amplifier

How to get that sound:
There's nothing very challenging here – use a humbucker in the neck position into an amplifier set for a light crunch (6/10) and add a little reverb.

Fascinating fact:
'My Sharona' was written for Sharona Alperin, The Knack singer Doug Fieger's girlfriend, and then only 17 years old and still in High School. She is now a highly successful real estate agent in the Los Angeles area and actively uses the song for marketing purposes (see *www.mysharona.com*). Sharona has also turned her hand to acting, and in 1999 she played a real estate agent in *Anywhere But Here* alongside Susan Sarandon and Natalie Portman.

Technical tips:
Use your 3rd or 4th finger to barre across the upper three strings in the C and B♭ chords, and use all down picks to give the riff an even punchier feel.

Most memorable lyric:
When you gonna give it to me, give it to me?
Is it just a matter of time, Sharona?
Is it just destiny, destiny?
Or is it just a game in my mind, Sharona?
Never gonna stop, give it up
Such a dirty mind
Always get it up for the
Touch of the younger kind
My my my ay-yai, woo!

© 1979 Eighties Music, Small Hill Music and Wise Brothers Music LLC, USA
BMG Music Publishing Ltd, London SW6 3JW and Campbell Connelly & Co Ltd, London W1D 3JB

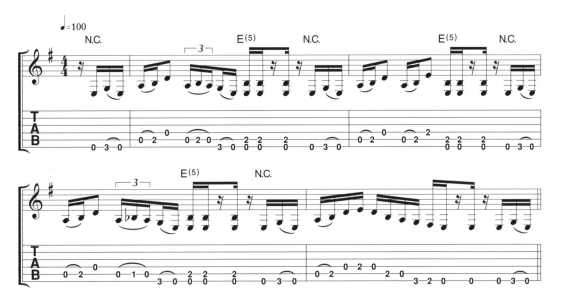

Words and music by:
Peter Green

From the album:
Then Play On (1969)

Highest chart placing (UK):
2 (1969)

Highest chart placing (US):
55 (1970)

Guitarist:
Peter Green

Set-up:
Steel string acoustic guitar

Fascinating facts:
The story of Peter's career is one of both tragedy and hope. He formed Fleetwood Mac back in 1967 with drummer Mick Fleetwood. In the space of only three short years he penned some enduring rock and blues classics such as 'Black Magic Woman', 'Oh Well', 'Albatross' and 'Need Your Love So Bad'.

His health rapidly declined as he descended into paranoid schizophrenia, the beginnings of which he is said to have written about in one of his last songs for Fleetwood Mac – 'The Green Manalishi (With The Two-Pronged Crown)'. He disappeared from the spotlight following an incident with a gun and an accountant (although you don't really need to be ill to find yourself in such a position!).

Despite some work in the early 80s as health permitted, the next time many people saw Peter was on a television documentary, he had gained a lot of weight, was still struggling mentally, and his fingernails were more than two inches long. Fortunately, with the help of his friends and colleagues he's been making a comeback both musically and physically, and his group, Peter Green's Splinter Group, are now performing and recording regularly.

In 1998 Peter was inducted into the *Rock And Roll Hall Of Fame* by fellow guitarist and admirer Carlos Santana. That night he appeared on stage with the rest of Fleetwood Mac.

In 2003, the current Fleetwood Mac line-up comprising of Stevie Nicks, Lindsey Buckingham, John McVie and Mick Fleetwood, released *Say You Will*, their first studio album since *Tango In The Night* (1987).

Most memorable lyric:
I can't help it about the shape I'm in
I can't sing
I ain't pretty
And my legs are thin.
But don't ask me what I think of you
I might not give you answers
That you want me to.

© 1970 Palan Music Publishing Ltd, London W1F 0LQ

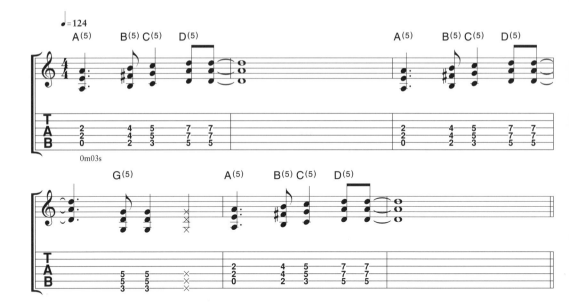

Words and music by:
Jon Anderson, Trevor Rabin, Chris Squire and Trevor Horn

From the album:
90125 (1983)

Highest chart placing (UK):
28 (1983)

Highest chart placing (US):
1 (1983)

Guitarist:
Trevor Rabin

Set-up:
Fender Stratocaster through a Marshall 50 watt stack

How to get that sound:
Trevor used a Fender Stratocaster fitted with a Dimarzio humbucker in the bridge position, which is responsible for the hard edged tone in the intro. The distorion is highly saturated so set your amp gain to 9 or 10/10. Add plenty of compression and digital ambient reverb, set the unit to a medium or large hall preset. There's also tonal shaping which probably wasn't carried out at the amp, a graphic E.Q. will produce the closest result.

Fascinating fact:
Since leaving Yes, Trevor has established himself as a very successful film composer. He was responsible for *The Glimmer Man, Con Air, Armageddon, Enemy Of The State, Deep Blue Sea, Remember The Titans* and *Gone In 60 Seconds.*

Most memorable lyric:
Move yourself
You always live your life
Never thinking of the future
Prove yourself
You are the move you make
Take your chances win or loser.

© 1983 Opio Publishing, Tremander Songs, Carlin Music Corp and Unforgettable Songs Ltd Warner/Chappell North America Ltd, London W6 8BS, Carlin Music Corp, London NW1 8BD and Unforgettable Songs Ltd, London W11 1DG

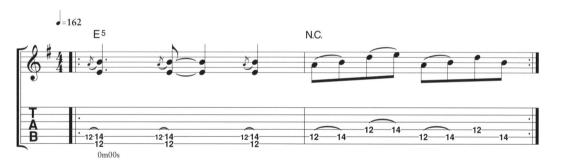

Words and music by:
John Osbourne, William Ward, Terrence Butler and Tony Iommi

From the album:
Paranoid (1970)

Highest chart placing (UK):
4 (1970)

Highest chart placing (US):
61 (1970)

Guitarist:
Tony Iommi

Set-up:
Gibson SG through a Laney stack

How to get that sound:
This is essentially the same sound as used on 'Iron Man' (page 56), with the difference in sound being down to room ambience, microphone placement and mix down factors such as E.Q. and panning.

Fascinating fact:
Following the accident that lead to Tony having the tips severed from two fingers (see page 56 – 'Iron Man') Tony's doctor was pessimistic about his chances of becoming an effective guitarist again. In an effort to console him, a friend gave Tony an album by the gypsy jazz guitarist Django Reinhardt, whose left hand was badly burned in a caravan fire, mis-shaping and fusing two fingers together. Django's playing inspired Tony to continue playing but not, curiously, to play jazz, leaving us to wonder what Sabbath would have sounded like had circumstances been different.

Most memorable lyric:
Finished with my woman 'cause she
Couldn't help me with my mind
People think I'm insane because
I am frowning all the time
All day long I think of things but
Nothing seems to satisfy
Think I'll lose my mind if I don't
Find something to pacify.

Can you help me
Occupy my brain?
Oh yeah.

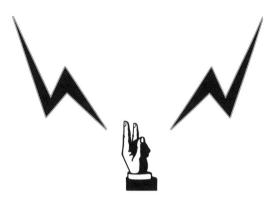

'Being mean and frightening just came naturally. When Ozzy sang, we made that sort of sound' Tony Iommi

© 1970 Westminster Music Ltd, London SW10 0SZ

83

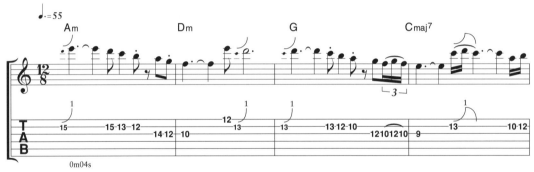

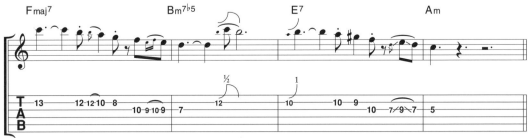

Words and music by:
Philip Lynott and Gary Moore

From the album:
Back On The Streets (1978)

Highest chart placing (UK):
8 (1979)

Guitarist:
Gary Moore

Set-up:
Gibson Les Paul through a Marshall stack

How to get that sound:
One effective way to get this tone is to select the neck pickup only on a Les Paul and set the tone to zero. Gain should be set quite high at about 8/10. Gary himself has stated that he doesn't use this method, instead he boosts the signal with an Ibanez Tube Screamer, which compresses the sound and reduces the high frequencies.

Fascinating fact:
Peter Green sold Gary his famous 1959 Gibson Les Paul. In 1996 Gary recorded a tribute album called *Blues for Greeny*. (See page 81 – 'Oh Well').

Gary often used this track to showcase the feedback or 'infinite' sustain trick. By standing close to the speaker cab or monitors it's possible to keep a note ringing on indefinitely (well, until you get bored anyway). The pitch coming from the speakers is (obviously!) the same as the pitch of the string, and so the string rings on in sympathy. Some pitches work better than others – it all depends on your guitar, your strings, where you stand, and how loud the amp is. It's also possible to completely lose it and break out into violent feedback, but often a subtle repositioning of guitar in relation to the speaker will bring the note right back out again. With a little practice it's possible to give the rest of the band a convenient mid-set 'comfort' break – in much the same way as 'Moby Dick' was used by Led Zeppelin.

Most memorable lyric:
I remember Paris in '49
The Champs Elysées, San Michelle
And old Beaujolais wine
And I recall that you were mine
In those Parisienne days.

© 1978 Maxwood Music Ltd, London NW1 0AD

Gtr. 1

Em

Gtr. 2*

0m00s
Tune down a semitone
* Kybds. & Bass arr. for Gtr.

Words and music by:
Hugh Cornwell, Jean-Jacques Burnel, Brian Duffy and David Greenfield

From the album:
Rattus Norvegicus (1977)

Highest chart placing (UK):
8 (1977)

Guitarist:
Hugh Cornwell

Set-up:
Fender Telecaster

How to get that sound:
Hugh's Telecaster has two single coil pickups, so if you haven't got a Tele use a Strat. The output from these guitars is hardly standard, so you should experiment with pickup selection as your results are likely to be wildly different.
The best way to replicate the distortion is with an effects pedal rather than at the amplifier – Hugh's sound almost borders on fuzz. Whichever method you choose you're unlikely to need more than about 7/10 gain or distortion. Finally, add a deep chorus or flange effect with a slow sweep.

Fascinating fact:
'Peaches' was banned by the BBC – not something that was terribly difficult to do at the time. The *Beeb* found the 'woman baiting' lyrics offensive, along with the use of the word 'clitoris' – despite this 'Peaches' made it into the UK Top 10, a feat they would later replicate with the songs 'No More Heroes' and 'Something Better Change'.

Technical tips:
The guitar part here shows only the top few notes of the chord that Hugh is actually using – the full chord is an Em chord at the 7th fret (x79987 for all you TAB aficionados). Play the chords with an upstroke and try to get a good attack in the tone – it may be inspired by reggae but it's still punk. Don't be overly concerned about how many strings you're striking, that's not important – it would be different every time Hugh played it himself.

Most memorable lyric:
Will you just take a look over there?
Where?
There!
Is she trying to get out of that clitoris
Liberation for women
That's what I preach
Preacher man
Walking on the beaches
Looking at the peaches ...

P

© 1976 Albion Music Ltd
Complete Music Ltd, London SW6 3JH

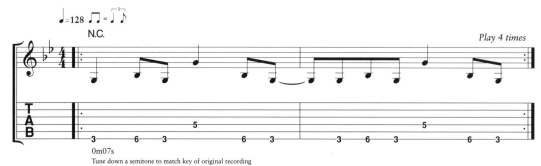

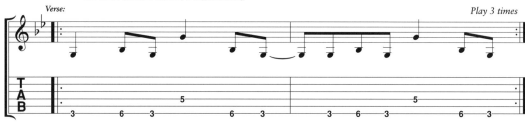

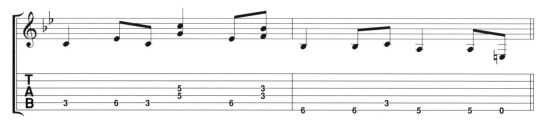

Words and music by:
Martin Gore

From the album:
Violator (1990)

Highest chart placing (UK):
13 (1989)

Highest chart placing (US):
28 (1990)

Guitarist:
Martin Gore

Set-up:
Gretsch Anniversary Guitar

How to get that sound:
Nothing short of a fat semi is going to produce the right tone for this track. The late Dick Knight, luthier to stars such as Dave Gilmour, Paul McCartney and Pete Townshend, made a copy of Martin's Gretsch and modified it to cut down on stage feedback. In the studio, however, Martin would have used the original guitar.

Technical tips:
The secret to playing this song well is in how you use the pick – twang it hard!

Most memorable lyric:
Reach out and touch me!
Your own
Personal
Jesus
Someone to hear your prayers
Someone who cares
Your own
Personal
Jesus
Someone to hear your prayers
Someone who's there.

© 1989 Grabbing Hands Music Ltd
EMI Music Publishing Ltd, London WC2H 0QY

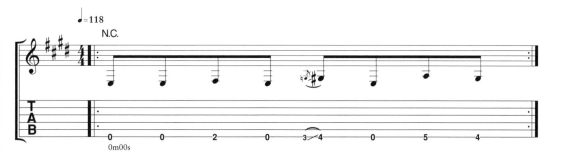

Music by:
Henry Mancini

Music by:
Henry Mancini

From the album:
Music From Peter Gunn (1959)

Highest chart placing (UK):
6 (1959)

Highest chart placing (US):
27 (1960)

Guitarist:
Duane Eddy

Set-up:
Gretsch *Chet Atkins* 6120

How to get that sound:
This is another track that is difficult to reproduce unless you've got something at least approaching the original instrument. The woody tones and sustain profile of a fat bodied semi-acoustic simply can't be faked on the likes of a Strat or a Les Paul. Another factor is that the pickups on old Gretsch instruments have a substantially different tone and output to more modern instruments, which are optimised for rock and pop music. In contrast, amplifier selection is far less critcal, a simple clean setting with some spring reverb will suffice.
A real Gretsch *Chet Atkins* 6120 is an expensive piece of wood by any calculation, but there are numerous cheaper semi-acoustics made by manufacturers such as Epiphone that with little effort can get close to the sound of artists like Duane Eddy, Chet Atkins, Brian Setzer, George Harrison and Martin Gore (see page left – 'Personal Jesus').

Fascinating fact:
This track became a Top 10 hit in the UK a second time when pop innovators The Art Of Noise, spearheaded by producer Trevor Horn, released a reworked version featuring the familiar twang of Duane's guitar. It even received a grammy for *Best Rock Instrumental* and introduced a whole new audience to Duane's music.

Technical tips:
Play all the notes with down strokes and don't be afraid to sit behind the beat a little. It may sound like the guitar is muted on the original recording, but that's just the sharp attack of the strings in contrast to the short sustain of the instrument.

P

© 1958 Northridge Music Co, USA
Worldwide print rights controlled by Warner Bros. Publications Inc/IMP Ltd

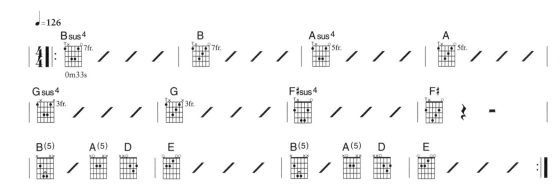

Words and music by:
Peter Townshend

From the album:
Tommy (1969)

Highest chart placing (UK):
4 (1969)

Highest chart placing (US):
19 (1969)

Guitarist:
Pete Townshend

Set-up:
Gibson J-200 steel string acoustic guitar

How to get that sound:
Much of the acoustic guitar tone on 'Pinball Wizard' is down to the recording, which is quite thin (possibly due to off-axis microphone placement) but at the same time captures the fantastic bell like ringing tone of Pete's J-200.
Use a light pick and strum quite close to the bridge to emphasize the pick attack and reduce the lower 'boomy' tones that are more prevalent if you record a guitar with the mic pointing straight at the soundhole.

Fascinating fact:
'Pinball Wizard' was inspired by Nik Cohn's book *Arfur Teenage Pinball Queen*. Fortunately for rock history, Pete must have discarded the idea of penning an opus based on one of Nik Cohn's other books, *Awopbopaloobop Alopbamboom*.

Technical tips:
The root notes of the descending chord pattern are all played by the thumb reaching over the top of the neck. This is easier if you've got what one of my ex-girlfriends used to call 'big hands'.

Most memorable lyric:
Ever since I was a young boy
I've played the silver ball
From Soho down to Brighton
I must have played them all
But I ain't seen nothing like him
In any amusement hall
That deaf, dumb and blind kid
Sure plays a mean pinball!

© 1969 Fabulous Music Ltd, London SW10 0SZ

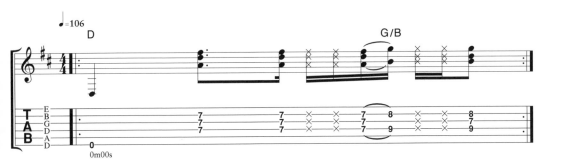

Words and music by:
Gary Stringer, John Bessant, Dominic Greensmith and Kenwyn House

From the album:
Glow (1997)

Highest chart placing (UK):
6 (1996)

Guitarist:
Kenwyn House

Set-up:
Fender Stratocaster through a Matchless Chieftain

How to get that sound:
The distortion is best achieved with a pedal such as a Big Muff – it's a sharper and tighter clip than a fuzz pedal, and would be difficult to reproduce simply by overdriving an amplifier. Set a Strat with a five position switch to the fourth position to bring in the warmer tones of the middle and neck pickups, while maintaining some bite at the top end. Leave the volume and tone controls fully open.

Fascinating fact:
Reef fell out with *TFI Friday* presenter Chris Evans after he persisted in playing an adaption of the song that the band had recorded to accompany the 'It's Your Letters' section of the show. They gave permission for the song to be played only once during a show on which they were appearing, but it was subsequently used every week despite protests from the band. The situation wasn't helped by fans who would regularly shout out 'It's Your Letters' as a request during live shows.

Technical tips:
The notes with cross noteheads are played by relaxing finger pressure in the fretting hand – don't try doing any palm muting here. The strumming direction is strictly alternate whether you're playing a note on any particular 16th note or not, and initially it's worth doing a few 'ghost' strums – i.e. not actually striking the strings but keeping the alternation going throughout.

Most memorable lyric:
So place your hands on my hope
Run your fingers through my soul
And the way that I feel right now
Oh Lord it may go.

P

© 1996 Warner/Chappell Music Ltd, London W6 8BS

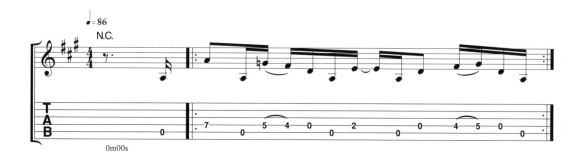

Words and music by:
Carole King and Gerry Goffin

From the album:
Pisces, Aquarius, Capricorn & Jones Ltd.
(1967)

Highest chart placing (UK):
11 (1967)

Highest chart placing (US):
3 (1967)

Guitarist:
Michael Nesmith

Set-up:
Gretsh semi-acoustic through a Vox amplifer

How to get that sound:
It's impossible to say exactly which instrument was used to play this riff, but it was probably a Gretsch Country Classic. All the more reason to buy a fat semi-acoustic (if you don't already own one) – just like 'Personal Jesus' and 'Peter Gunn Theme', there's really no other way of getting that big woody tone.
Gretsch also manufactured a special Monkees signature model, the Gretsch 6123 *Monkees*, available only in the same red colour as Michael's Country Classic, and with a Monkees logo on the pick guard.

Fascinating fact:
Most people have heard that The Monkees didn't play the instruments on their earlier albums, and this is partly true with the exception being Michael Nesmith. Michael was an accomplished guitarist and songwriter, and while he didn't perform on every song, session notes show that this is one on which he did. Session musicians were generally called on to perform non-vocal duties, and included musicians as diverse as (brace yourself!) Neil Young and Ry Cooder, who both played on 'As We Go Along' from The Monkees film *Head* amongst others.

Most memorable lyric:
Another Pleasant Valley Sunday
Here in status symbol land
Mothers complain about how hard life is
And the kids just don't understand.

© 1967 Screen Gems-EMI Music Ltd, London WC2H 0QY

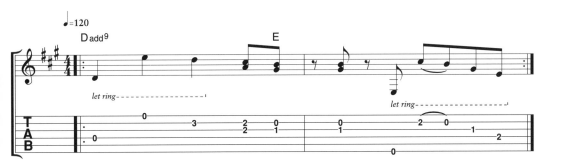

Words and music by:
David Bowie

From the album:
Diamond Dogs (1974)

Highest chart placing (UK):
5 (1974)

Highest chart placing (US):
64 (1974)

Guitarist:
Mick Ronson

Set-up:
1968 Gibson Les Paul Custom through a Marshall stack

How to get that sound:
This is a very similar sound to Mick's playing on the track 'Jean Genie' (see page 59), once again demonstrating the use of a fixed wah – switching on the wah pedal and leaving it in one position to boost certain frequencies, usually in the mid range. The fuzz effect was probably produced with a Vox Tone Bender pedal.

Fuzz is a distinctive hard clipping distortion effect, and if you're into the sounds of the 60s and 70s you'd be well advised to get your hands on either an original, or one of the many reissued units such as the Fuzz Face. Now made by Dunlop, the original Dallas Arbiter unit was much favoured by Jimi Hendrix.

Mick had the paint and varnish removed from his Les Paul because he'd heard that it would improve the tone by making it more 'edgy'. By the time the signal had run through the fuzz and wah it's doubtful that anyone could hear difference.

Technical tips:
Play the first double stop with your second and third fingers rather than with a barre. This makes it easier to play the following note with your first finger.

Most memorable lyric:
Doo doo doo-doo doo doo doo doo
Doo doo doo-doo doo doo doo doo
Doo doo doo-doo doo doo doo doo

Got your mother in a whirl
She's not sure if you're a boy or a girl
Hey, babe, your hair's alright
Hey, babe, lets go out tonight
You like me, and I like it all
We like dancing, and we look divine
You love bands when they play it hard
You want more, and you want it first
Put you down, say I'm wrong
You tacky thing, you put them on.

'[Rock music] is depressing and sterile and, ultimately, evil.' David Bowie

---

© 1974 EMI Music Publishing Ltd, Moth Music and Tintoretto Music
EMI Music Publishing Ltd, London WC2H 0QY, Chrysalis Music Ltd, London W10 6SP and RZO Music Ltd, London W1M 5FF

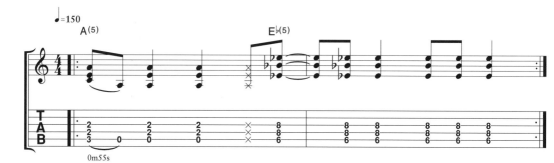

Words and music by:
Gareth Coombes, Daniel Goffey, Michael Quinn and Robert Coombes

From the album:
In It For The Money (1997)

Highest chart placing (UK):
2 (1997)

Guitarist:
Gaz Coombes

Set-up:
Gibson 335 through a Marshal 2x12 combo

How to get that sound:
Guitar selection isn't critical here, as the distortion levels have irradicated any trace of an identifiable guitar signature. Choose a guitar with humbuckers and switch it to the bridge position. Set the amplifier gain high – if you have a modern hi-gain amp you may only need to go up to 8/10 but others may well require 10/10. Don't let the signal saturate into death metal – it's very heavy but it's not over the top. Compression was probably added during mixing, but you could replicate a similar effect by adding a compressor in the effects loop – adding it before the pre-amp won't have the same effect. Interestingly, Gaz seems to favour a combo rather than the ubiquitous stack, but adds further 2x12 cabs for better sound dispersion.

Fascinating fact:
Danny Goffey, the Supergrass drummer, used to play in a band called The Fallopian Tubes, who performed songs such as 'My Wife Shut My Gonads In The Door'.

Technical tips:
Keep your strumming hand moving throughout, play down strums on the downbeats and up strums on the upbeats. This keeps the strumming pattern fluid and avoids any jerky start/stop movements that are more difficult to keep in time.

Most memorable lyric:
Got it today, what a day, thanks a million!
Spent too much time wondering
Why I got a feeling
I know you wanna try to get away,
But it's the hardest thing
You'll ever know.

R

                    © 1996 EMI Music Publishing Ltd, London WC2H 0QY

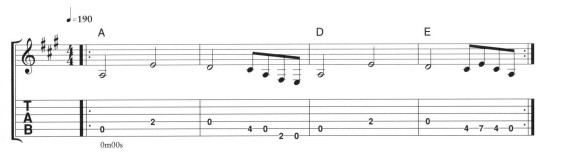

Words and music by:
Mark Hoppus, Tom DeLonge and Travis Barker

From the album:
Take Off Your Pants And Jacket (2001)

Highest chart placing (UK):
14 (2001)

Highest chart placing (US):
71 (2001)

Guitarist:
Tom DeLonge

Set-up:
Fender Stratocaster

How to get that sound:
Set the guitar to use the bridge pickup and leave the controls wide open. Start with your amplifier's gain set to about 7/10 and work from there. Listen to the recording, you can still hear a certain Stratocaster 'twang' in the eighth note runs at the end of each bar – you've got too much gain when that starts to disappear.

Fascinating fact:
The title of the album is a play on words which could be read *Take Off Your Pants And Jack It*. Please don't ask me to explain any further.

Technical tips:
This is another excellent riff for beginners – it's quite a fast tempo but very straight forward. Play the last four notes of bars two and four with alternate picking (down-up-down-up).

Most memorable lyric:
'Cause I fell in love
With the girl at the rock show
She said what?
And I told her that I didn't know
She's so cool
Gonna sneak in
Through her window
Everything's better
When she's around
I can't wait
'Til her parents go out of town
I fell in love
With the girl at the rock show.

© 2001 Fun With Goats, USA
EMI Music Publishing Ltd, London WC2H 0QY

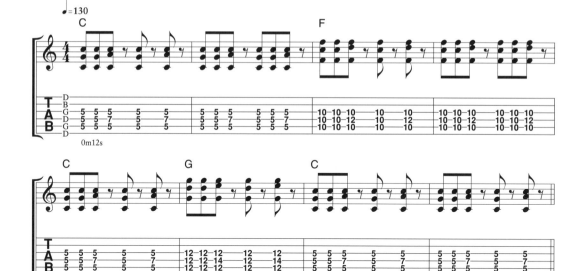

***

Words and music by:
John Fogerty

From the album:
Rockin' All Over The World (1977)

Highest chart placing (UK):
3 (1977)

R

Guitarists:
Francis Rossi
Rick Parfitt

Set-up:
Fender Telecaster through Vox AC30

How to get that sound:
The guitar sounds are fairly typical of what you get simply by plugging a Telecaster into an AC30. If you have a modelling amplifier or effects unit head straight for the AC30 patches.

Fascinating fact:
In 1983, tension had been building in the band between the bassist Alan Lancaster and guitarists Francis Rossi and Rick Parfitt. Despite still being an official member of the group, Alan headed off to set up home in Australia. In his absence the ever innovative Quo decided to deploy a cardboard cutout of Alan for several television appearances and a video.

Most memorable lyric:
And I like it, I like it, I like it, I like it
I li-li-li-like it, li-li-li-like it
Here we go
Rockin' all over the world.

© 1975 Wenaha Music Company, USA
Hornall Brothers Music Ltd, London SW6 5SH

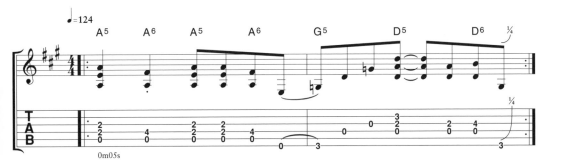

© 1993 EMI Music Publishing Ltd, London WC2H 0QY and Complete Music Ltd, London SW6 3JH

Words and music by:
Bobby Gillespie, Robert Young and Andrew Innes

From the album:
Give Out But Don't Give Up (1994)

Highest chart placing (UK):
7 (1994)

Guitarists:
Andrew Innes
Robert Young

Set-up:
Gibson Les Paul through a Marshall stack

How to get that sound:
The guitars on this track are sharper and thinner than you'd expect to get from tube overdrive – warmth and depth have been sacrificed for a cutting attack and glassy presence.
Select the bridge pickup on your guitar and run it through a distortion pedal. Avoid using modern hi-gain pedals – instead opt for an older model such as the Ibanez TS-9 tube screamer, which has the added effect of compressing the signal slightly. Gain settings will depend on the output level of your pickups, but it's unlikely you'll need to go much beyond about 6/10. A slight midrange boost can be achieved with the pedal's tone control.

Technical tips:
Here's a small but significant point: the staccato on the second beat of the first bar is achieved by damping – after you strike the notes with the pick quickly place the side of your hand on the strings to completely deaden the sound. Both pick and damp should take place in one smooth movement.

Most memorable lyric:
Get your rocks off
Get your rocks off honey
Shake it now now
Get 'em off downtown
Get your rocks off
Get you rocks off honey
Shake it now now
Get 'em off downtown.

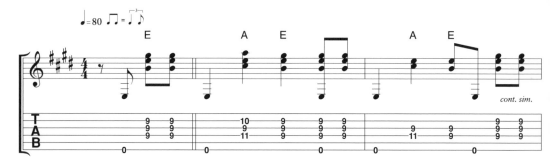

Words and music by:
Joe Walsh, J. Vitale, Kenny Passarelli and R. Grace

From the album:
The Smoker You Drink, The Player You Get (1973)

Highest chart placing (UK):
39 (1977)

Highest chart placing (US):
23 (1973)

Guitarist:
Joe Walsh

Set-up:
Gibson Les Paul through a Fender Super Reverb

How to get that sound:
The distortion on this track verges on fuzz, but has a tube-like warmth that suggests it's mainly pre-amp gain. Joe is fond of carrying out his own modifications to amplifiers and effects units, removing a resistor here and there, and he sometimes even runs his guitar through an echo unit that isn't activated to get the treble boost supplied by the effects bypass electronics. Essentially this means that his guitar signal is likely to be arriving at the amp a lot 'hotter' than usual, and this has a resultant effect on the amplifier's distortion character. Joe's bypassed echo unit provides a boost effect much like that provided by the Dallas Arbiter Rangemaster or Brian May's 'treble booster'.
You can get close to this sound with a Les Paul and a fuzz box set for a light clip, and then be careful not to lose the rich tone in the low end. Pan the mix fully left to hear the guitar on its own.

Fascinating fact:
The talk box solo on *Rocky Mountain High* is one of Joe's favourites, and inspired Peter Frampton to adopt the effect.

Most memorable lyric:
Spent the last year
Rocky Mountain Way
Couldn't get much higher
Out to pasture
Think it's safe to say
Time to open fire
And we don't need the ladies
Crying 'cause the story's sad
'Cause the Rocky Mountain Way
Is better than the way we had.

© 1973 ABC Dunhill Music Inc and Barn Storm Music Inc, USA
Universal/MCA Music Ltd, London W6 8JA

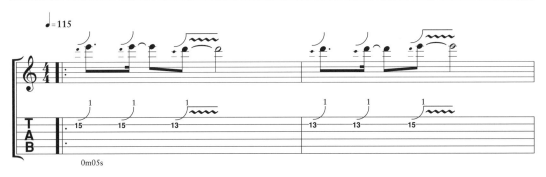

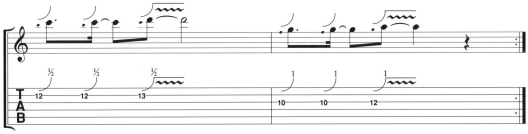

Words and music by:
Stephen Harris

From the album:
The Number Of The Beast (1982)

Highest chart placing (UK):
7 (1982)

Guitarists:
Dave Murray
Adrian Smith

Set-up:
Fender Stratocaster through a Marshall stack

How to get that sound:
Use a guitar with a single coil pickup in the neck position, and select that pickup on its own. Set up a smooth but saturated tube overdrive at the amplifier and counter it by rolling off most of the tone at the guitar. Dial the tone control down as low as 0/10 if necessary. The addition of a little compression will knock the edge off of the attack by reducing pick noise and the natural decay of the strings.
A similar approach using a Gibson Les Paul's neck pickup will produce the 'Sweet Child O' Mine' (Guns 'N' Roses) tonal signature.

Fascinating fact:
While singing for his former band Samson, Maiden vocalist Bruce Dickinson accidentally shattered a huge glass globe with a single piercing scream during a gig at Chelsea College. Such destruction relies on singing the exact same resonant pitch as the 'target'. Thereafter Bruce was nicknamed 'Air Raid Siren'.

Most memorable lyric:
White man came
Across the sea
He brought us pain
And misery
He killed our tribes
He killed our creed
He took our game
For his own need.

R

© 1982 Zomba Music Publishers Ltd, London SW6 3JW

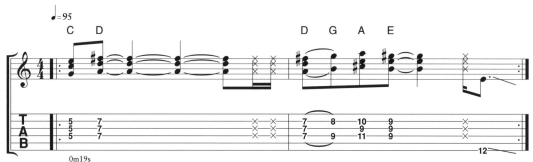

0m19s

Tune guitar down a semitone to match key of original recording

Words and music by:
Edward Van Halen, Alex Van Halen, Michael Anthony and David Lee Roth

From the album:
Van Halen (1978)

Guitarist:
Eddie Van Halen

Set-up:
Customised 'Frankenstrat' though a Marshall stack

How to get that sound:
The signature guitar sound from the debut *Van Halen* album is well described elsewhere in this book (See Page 10 – 'Ain't Talkin' 'Bout Love' and Page 36 – 'Eruption'). For this riff Eddie didn't use any effects other than reverb.

Note how Eddie gets a cleaner tone during the verses by backing off the volume control at the guitar. This trick was often adopted before channel switching became a standard feature on amplifiers, and is a great way of getting a lightly overdriven tone that is sensitive to the attack of the guitar, play hard and you break into overdrive, play softly and you're rewarded with a warm clean tone. This is one of the many differences between valve amplifiers and their solid state counterparts, and partly explains why the music industry is one of the very last to hold on to what has otherwise become a redundant technology.

Another goody from Eddie's trick bag can be heard before this riff plays for the first time in the intro. The very high dulcimer-like string noise is achieved by strumming the strings upwards between the tuning posts and the nut. However, you'll get a different 'chord' unless your headstock is of the same design as Eddie's and you use the same gauge strings!

Fascinating fact:
Eddie is very protective of some of the special techniques that he uses, and would often infuriate guitarists who attended his gigs by turning his back on the audience during his solos.

Most memorable lyric:
I found a simple life wasn't simple
When I jumped out on that road
Ain't got no love, no love you'd call real
Ain't got nobody waiting at home.

© 1978 Van Halen Music and Diamond Dave Music, USA
Warner/Chappell Music Ltd, London W6 8BS and Chrysalis Music Ltd, London W10 6SP

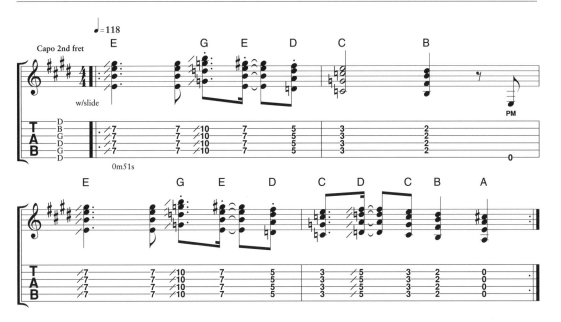

Words and music by:
Jack White

From the album:
Elephant (2003)

Highest chart placing (UK):
7 (2003)

Highest chart placing (US):
76 (2003)

Guitarist:
Jack White

Set-up:
Airline through a Sears Silvertone 100 watt

How to get that sound:
Start with a moderate crunchy tone by setting the amplifier gain to about 6/10. Tube amplifiers from manufacturers such as Sears and Orange have a glassy top end that you can emulate to some extent by adding presence or treble boost. If you have a modelling amp or effects unit switch it to a Vox or Orange model and add a little reverb – no more than 2/10 – and experiment with cabinet emulation if it's available. Select the bridge pickup and leave the guitar controls wide open. The whole song is played with a bottleneck.

Most memorable lyric:
I'm gonna fight 'em off
A seven nation army couldn't hold me back
They're gonna rip it off
Taking their time right behind my back.

© 2003 Peppermint Stripe Music, USA
EMI Music Publishing Ltd, London WC2H 0QY

♩ = 135

N.C.

0m18s

Words and music by:
Ian Astbury and William Duffy

From the album:
Love (1985)

Highest chart placing (UK):
15 (1985)

Guitarist:
William H. Duffy

Set-up:
Gretsch White Falcon through a Roland JC-120
Jazz Chorus amplifier

How to get that sound:
Time to dust off your analogue distortion pedals! A
good place to start would be the Boss SD-1 Super
Overdrive or the Ibanez TS-9 Tube Screamer. You
should also rummage around for any old Boss
delay pedals as Duffy swears they're the key to the
authentic 'She Sells Sanctuary' sound.
You should be able to get quite close straight away
by plugging in a semi-acoustic with the bridge
pickup selected through the pedals with the
distortion set at about 7/10.

Fascinating fact:
The Roland JC-120 Jazz Chorus, which was used
extensively on the *Love* album, is still on sale
today. It's fallen a little out of fashion due to a
move away from solid state electronics in favour of
both vintage tube designs and modern digital
technology. While it has a devoted user base it also
has its detractors, see page 130 – 'What Difference
Does It Make?'. The Roland JC-120 is modelled in
both the Line 6 *Pod* and the Behringer *V-Amp*.

Most memorable lyric:
Oh the heads that turn
Make my back burn
And those heads that turn
Make my back
Make my back burn.

The sparkle in your eyes
Keeps me alive
And the sparkle in your eyes
Keeps me alive
Keeps me alive.

The world
And the world turns around
The world
The world yeah
The world drags me down.

S

© 1986 Tayminster Ltd and Screenchoice Ltd
Chappell Music Ltd, London W6 8BS

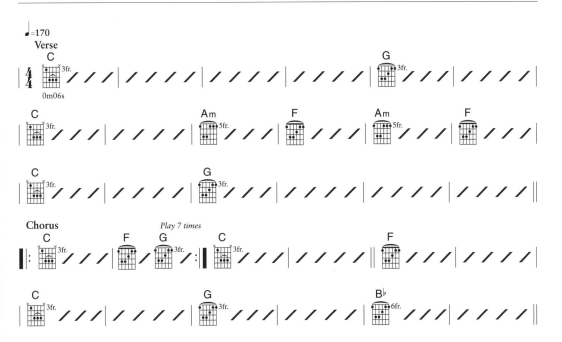

Words and music by:
Thomas Erdelyi, John Cummings, Jeffrey Hyman and Douglas Calvin

From the album:
Rocket To Russia (1977)

Highest chart placing (UK):
22 (1977)

Highest chart placing (US):
81 (1977)

Guitarist:
Johnny Ramone

Set-up:
Mosrite Venture II through a Marshall stack

How to get that sound:
This is straight-into-the-amp rock, just select the bridge pickup and adjust the gain to taste. Make sure the E.Q. doesn't emphasise the bottom end. The sound is fairly compressed, but this is likely to be the result of the mixing and mastering process. The Mosrite has a fairly distinctive sound despite all the distortion, check out other Mosrite players such as Wayne Kramer (MC5) for comparison.

Most memorable lyric:
Well the kids are all hopped up
And ready to go
They're ready to go now
They got their surfboards
And they're going to the discotheque
A-Go-Go
But she just couldn't stay
She had to break away
Well New York City really has it all
Oh yeah
Oh yeah!

© 1977 Taco Tunes and Bleu Disque Music Co Inc, USA
Warner/Chappell North America Ltd, London W6 8BS

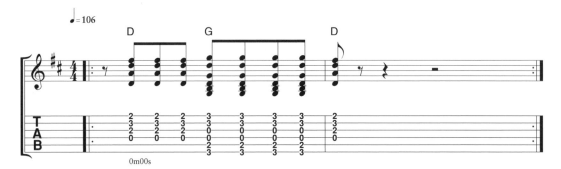

Words and music by:
Joe Strummer and Mick Jones

From the album:
Combat Rock (1982)

Highest chart placing (UK):
17 (1982)

Highest chart placing (UK):
45 (1982)

Guitarists:
Mick Jones
Joe Strummer

Set-up:
Fender Telecaster through a Music Man amplifier

How to get that sound:
The basic guitar sound is a no-frills overdriven Telecaster with the bridge pickup selected. Set the gain to around 8/10 – if you have amp modelling effects choose a vintage patch such as the Vox AC30 and then experiment with cabinet emulation if available.

Listen carefully to the basic guitar sound by panning your hi-fi hard right – after the first few bars the riff is double tracked and panned to opposite sides. Some delay and multi-effects units have an ADT (automatic double tracking) setting which can be useful for recreating double tracking in a live situation, but for recording purposes the end result is always better if actually recording another part. It's also possible to get something similar by setting a delay unit to play a single 'clone' a fraction of a second later, in a stereo unit you can further enhance this by adjusting the tone and character of one of the signals.

Fascinating fact:
Joe was arrested in 1980 for attacking a fan with his guitar after a fight erupted at a concert in Hamburg, Germany.

Most memorable lyric:
Darling you gotta let me know
Should I stay or should I go?
If you say that you are mine
I'll be here till the end of time
So you got to let me know
Should I stay or should I go?

© 1982 Nineden Ltd
Universal Music Publishing Ltd, London W6 8JA

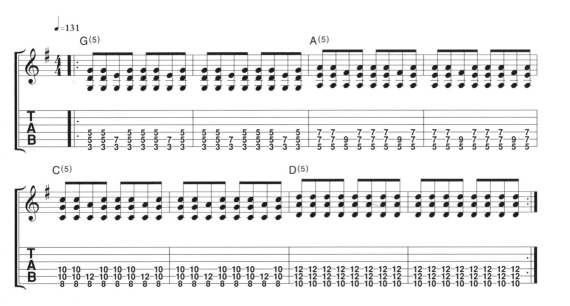

Words and music by:
David Brock and Bob Calvert

From the album:
Originally released only as a single, consequently added to numerous albums.

Highest chart placing (UK):
3 (1972)

Guitarist:
Dave Brock

Set-up:
Custom made Dick Knight 'Les Paul' through a HiWatt stack

How to get that sound:
There's not much mystery to replicating the main riff – select the bridge pickup and drive the amplifier hard with lots of gain. Remember that we're looking at a recording from 1972 here, so don't be tempted to wander into the realms of modern super saturation. Note that the recording has the vocals and guitars hard panned to opposite speakers – you can get a much clearer idea of the guitar parts and tone if you set the balance control on your hi-fi fully to the right. It's always worth checking out the instrument panning – listen to some early Van Halen and you'll see what I mean!

Fascinating fact:
Surprisingly, Dave Brock, the founding father of trippy space rock, started out playing the banjo in a New Orleans-style jazz band.

Most memorable lyric:
It flies sideways through time
It's an electric line
To your zodiac sign.

It flies out of a dream
It's anti-septically clean
You're gonna know where I've been
In my silver machine.

S

© 1972 EMI United Partnership Ltd, USA
Worldwide print rights controlled by Warner Bros. Publications Inc/IMP Ltd

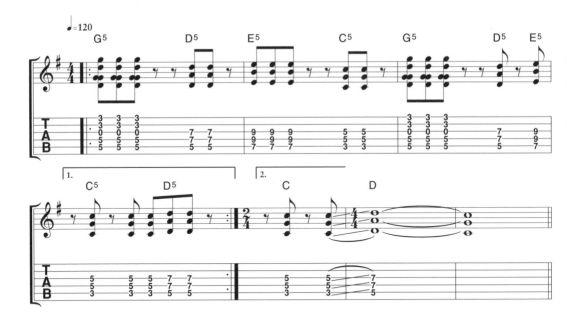

Words and music by:
Russell Ballard

From the album:
Down To Earth (1979)

Highest chart placing (UK):
6 (1979)

Guitarist:
Ritchie Blackmore

Set-up:
Fender Stratocaster through a Marshall stack

How to get that sound:
The guitar sound on this track is pure Stratocaster into overdriven Marshall. Use the bridge pickup and dial in about 8/10 of vintage gain.

Fascinating fact:
Ritchie's Strats have scalloped fingerboards – in this procedure a small amount of wood is scooped out between the frets creating a much greater space between the fingerboard and strings. This facilitates string bending and vibrato, and even allows sitar-like string bending, but such instruments are notoriously difficult to keep in tune. Other players who favour this treatment are

K.K. Downing (Judas Priest), Yngwie Malmsteen and John McLaughlin. Fender have manufactured two versions of the Stratocaster featuring scallop profiled necks, the Ritchie Blackmore and Yngwie Malmsteen signature models.

Most memorable lyric:
I get the same old dreams
Same time every night
Fall to the ground and I wake up
So I get out of bed
Put on my shoes
And in my head
Thoughts fly back to the break-up
These four walls are closing in
Look at the fix you put me in.

Since you've been gone
Since you've been gone
I'm out of my head can't take it
Could I be wrong
But since you've been gone
You cast a spell, so break it.

© 1976 Russell Ballard Ltd
Complete Music Ltd, London SW6 3JH

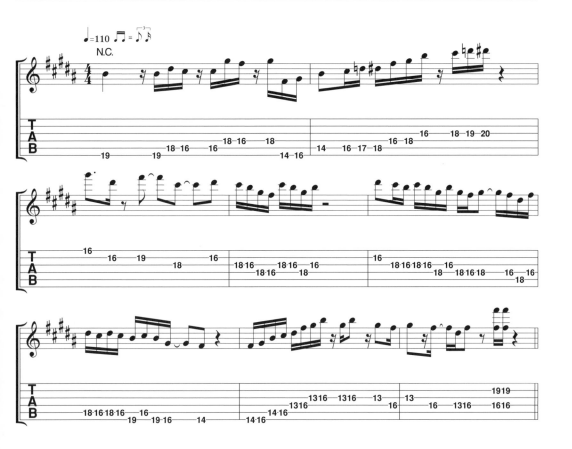

Words and music by:
Stevie Wonder

From the album:
Songs In The Key Of Life (1976)

Highest chart placing (UK):
2 (1977)

Highest chart placing (US):
1 (1977)

Guitarist:
Mike Sembello

Fascinating fact:
Mike is a prolific session musician and producer and has worked with numerous top stars such as Michael Jackson and Diana Ross. His most famous work however is probably 'Maniac', the song he penned for the 1983 movie *Flashdance*.

Technical tips:
Blow the dust off your metronome, you're going to need it. This is a tricky but very satisfying melodic line to play. The majority of it is in the key of B major pentatonic, but many guitarists will prefer to think of it as the basic G sharp minor pentatonic box shape. If you're seriously attempting to play this then you're probably a fairly proficient player and already adjusting where on the neck you want to play the notes. That's fine, it's the notes and feel that are important, and position is not critical as there are no hammer-ons and pull-offs to worry about - you're free to play the riff where it makes the most sense to you on the fretboard.

Most memorable lyric:
Music is a world within itself
With a language we all understand
With an equal opportunity
For all to sing, dance and clap their hands
But just because a record has a groove
Don't make it in the groove
But you can tell right away at letter A
When the people start to move.

© 1976 Black Bull Music Inc and Jobete Music Co Inc, USA
Black Bull Music/Jobete Music (UK) Ltd, London WC2H 0QY

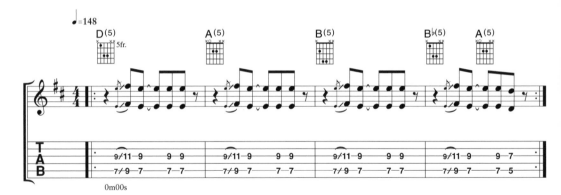

Words and music by:
Lauren Christy, David Alspach, Graham Edwards and Avril Lavigne

From the album:
Let's Go (2002)

Highest chart placing (UK):
8 (2002)

Highest chart placing (US):
10 (2002)

Guitarist:
Evan Taubenfeld

Set-up:
PRS Single Cut through a Mesa Boogie stack

How to get that sound:
Here's some slick super-saturated guitar to get your teeth into. Using the bridge guitar pickup and leaving the controls fully open, turn the amp gain into the red zone, shape the EQ with a graphic and add some compression. On the original recording this may have been added at the desk but it's quite possible to get close with pedal effects units. The octaves will produce a quite different distortion profile to playing only single notes, so play the actual riff when making adjustments to your sound.

Fascinating fact:
It's hard to imagine coming from the person whose job description is 'Musical Director' of Avril Lavigne's band, but Evan claims his guitar tech handles all the electronic stuff – he doesn't even know how to switch his amp on.

Technical tips:
If you haven't played octaves before, or you're experiencing unwanted sound from the other strings, then listen up. Use your first finger to play the lower note and rest the tip against the sixth (thickest) string to stop it from ringing. Instead of getting right up onto your finger tip, allow it to 'slouch' over the 4th string, deadening it in the process. So far we have one finger doing three jobs! Next up, your little (pinky) finger plays the higher note on the 3rd string. By utilising the same highly professional 'slouch' dampening technique you're able to dampen the top two strings, leaving you to strum away happily, safe in the knowledge that all the strings are covered.

Most memorable lyric:
He was a boy, she was a girl
Can I make it anymore obvious?
He was a punk, she did ballet
What more can I say?
He wanted her, she'd never tell
Secretly she wanted him as well.
But all of her friends stuck up their nose
They had a problem with his baggy clothes.

© 2002 Rainbow Fish Music, Ferry Hill Songs, Mr Spock Music and Almo-Music Corp, USA
Warner/Chappell North America Ltd, London W6 8BS and Rondor Music (London) Ltd, London W6 8JA

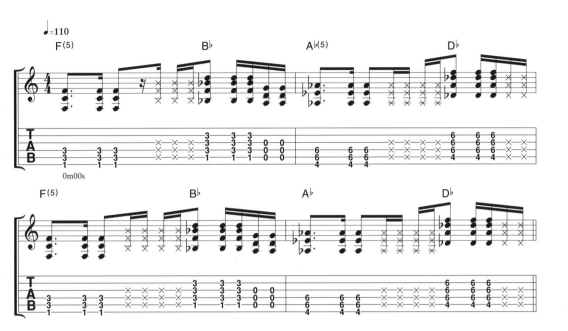

Words and music by:
Kurt Cobain, Chris Novoselic and David Grohl

From the album:
Nevermind (1991)

Highest chart placing (UK):
7 (1991)

Highest chart placing (US):
6 (1992)

Guitarist:
Kurt Cobain

Set-up:
Fender Jaguar through a Mesa/Boogie Studio .22 preamp, Crown power amp and Marshall cabinets

How to get that sound:
The tone is near-unadulterated Fender plus Boogie, shaped at the amp to emphasise the mid-frequencies. Use the guitar's bridge pickup and set the amp gain to a notch below the point at which clipping occurs. The Boogie .22 preamp features a 5 band graphic E.Q. which gives plenty of scope for tonal reshaping.

Fascinating fact:
The title of this track comes from an incident when Nirvana were drinking with a friend, Kathleen Hannah. After a while, they were all hopelessly drunk, and Kathleen wrote on the wall 'Kurt smells like teen spirit'. This was misinterpreted by Kurt as meaning that he was likely to start a huge teenage rebellion, whereas she actually meant that he smelled as though he had been using the deodorant, *Teen Spirit*.

Most memorable lyric:
Load up on guns and
Bring your friends
It's fun to lose
And to pretend
She's over bored
And self assured
Oh no, I know
A dirty word
Hello, hello, hello, how low?

With the lights out it's less dangerous
Here we are now, entertain us
I feel stupid, and contagious
Here we are now, entertain us.

S

© 1991 The End Of Music and EMI Virgin Songs Inc, USA
EMI Virgin Music Ltd, London WC2H 0QY

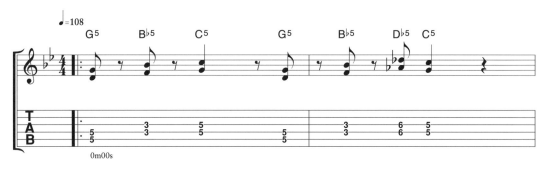

Words and music by:
Jon Lord, Ritchie Blackmore, Ian Gillan, Roger Glover and Ian Paice

From the album:
Machine Head (1972)

Highest chart placing (UK):
21 (1977)

Highest chart placing (US):
4 (1973)

Guitarist:
Ritchie Blackmore

Set-up:
Fender Stratocaster through a Marshall stack

Fascinating fact:
'Smoke On The Water' tells the story of an incident that happened when band members from Deep Purple attended a concert by Frank Zappa And The Mothers Of Invention at the Casino in Montreux, Switzerland. The band were booked to record the *Machine Head* album using the Rolling Stones mobile recording unit at the Casino in the days following the concert, but during the event 'some stupid with a flare gun' let off a round directly into the rattan-covered ceiling, sending the place up in a fireball, and destroying the entire casino along with all of the band's equipment. Amazingly no-one was killed.

Technical tips:
Ritchie doesn't use a pick to play the intro, he uses his thumb and index finger. If you listen closely to Ritchie playing the track you'll hear that the notes sound exactly together and don't have the sharp attack of a pick.

Curious covers:
Lying somewhere between remarkable and hilarious, Pat Boone's cover of 'Smoke On The Water' from his album *In A Metal Mood: No More Mr. Nice Guy* features a scorching guitar solo by Ritchie himself. Another cover song from the album, 'Crazy Train', was used as the theme tune to the fly-on-the-wall documentary of Ozzie Osbourne's daily life, *The Osbournes*.

Most memorable lyric:
We all came out to Montreux
On the Lake Geneva shoreline
To make records with a mobile
We didn't have much time
Frank Zappa and the Mothers
Were at the best place around
But some stupid with a flare gun
Burned the place to the ground.

© 1972 B Feldman & Co Ltd trading as Hec Music, London WC2H 0QY

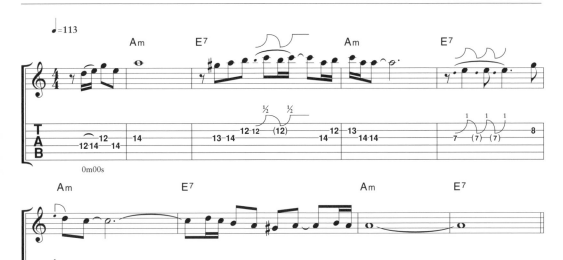

Words and music by:
Itaal Shur and Rob Thomas

From the album:
Supernatural (1999)

Highest chart placing (UK):
3 (2000)

Highest chart placing (US):
1 (1999)

Guitarist:
Carlos Santana

Set-up:
PRS Santana through a Mesa/Boogie

Most memorable lyric:
Man it's a hot one
Like seven inches from the midday sun
I hear you whisper
And the words melt everyone
But you stay so cool
My munequita, my Spanish Harlem Mona Lisa
You're my reason for reason
The step in my groove
And if you say this life ain't good enough
I would give my world to lift you up
I could change my life to better suit your mood
'Cause you're so smooth
And just like the ocean under the moon
Well it's the same as the emotion
That I get from you
You got the kind of lovin' that can be so smooth
Gimme your heart, make it real
Or else forget about it.

How to get that sound:
Despite the fact that Carlos Santana's signature tone is instantly recognizeable, he's been able to squeeze it from a number of different instruments over the years, including the Gibson Les Paul, Gibson SG, Yamaha SG 2000 and more recently the Paul Reed Smith *Santana* models I, II and III. All these guitars are thru-neck mahogany-bodied instruments with humbucking pickups. He often uses the much neglected neck pickup, and always uses a valve amplifier. If you don't own a Mesa/Boogie, patches appear in nearly all modelling F/X units.

© 1999 Itaal Shur Music and Bidnis Inc, USA
Warner/Chappell Music Ltd, London W6 8BS and EMI Music Publishing Ltd, London WC2H 0QY

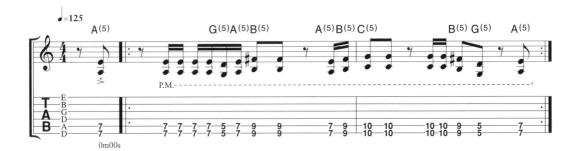

Words and music by:
Michael Jackson

From the album:
ANThology (2001)

Highest chart placing (UK):
3 (2001)

Highest chart placing (US):
23 (2001)

Guitarist:
Terence Corso

Set-up:
Paul Reed Smith CE 22 through a Marshall stack

How to get that sound:
Select the bridge pickup of a humbuckered guitar and saturate the distortion with gain of 9/10 or 10/10. Add a little compression.

Fascinating fact:
The Alien Ant Farm video of 'Smooth Criminal' is a light-hearted send up of Michael Jackson, the song's composer. Made with his full consent, it features a diapered pet chimp, moonwalkers and a hilariously unsubtle crotch grab.

Technical tips:
This is in drop D tuning, so you'll need to tune the low E string down a tone. Use the 4th string as reference, it's also a D but sounds an octave higher than the note you'll be tuning down to. Tuning this way facilitates fast power chord changes because they can be played with a simple barre.

Most memorable lyric:
As he came in through the window
With a sound of a crescendo
He came into her apartment
Left the bloodstains on the carpet
She was sitting at the table
He could see she was unable
So she ran into the bedroom
She was struck down
It was her doom.

© 1987 Mijac Music, USA
Warner Chappell Music Ltd, London W6 8BS

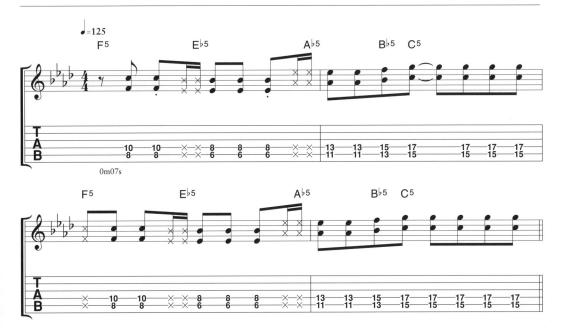

Words and music by:
Damon Albarn, Alex James, Graham Coxon and David Rowntree

From the album:
Blur (1997)

Highest chart placing (UK):
2 (1997)

Guitarist:
Graham Coxon

Set-up:
Fender Telecaster through a ... Marshall stack!?

How to get that sound:
Unbelieveable as it sounds, according to an article published at *grahamcoxon.com* the guitars on this song were played through "those toy Marshall amps". This could mean either the Marshall MS2 Mini Practice Amp, which is barely taller than a cigarette packet and would be dwarfed by a studio microphone, or perhaps even the Marshall MS4, the stack version of the MS2 which stands at a colossal 25cm tall. There's something a little *'Spinal Tap'* about this and I'm not sure that I believe it.

Most memorable lyric:
*I got my head checked
By a jumbo jet
It wasn't easy but nothing is
No ...*

Woo hoo!

*Well I feel heavy metal
And I'm pins and I'm needles
Well I lie and I'm easy
All of the time and I'm never sure
Why I need you
Pleased to meet you.*

© 1996 EMI Music Publishing Ltd, London WC2H 0QY

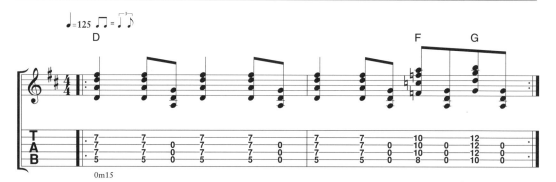

Words and music by:
Peter Hayes, Robert Been and Nicholas Jago

From the album:
Black Rebel Motorcycle Club (2001)

Highest chart placing (UK):
27 (2002)

Guitarists:
Peter Hayes
Robert Turner

Set-up:
Gibson ES-335 through Fender Twin amplifiers

How to get that sound:
Feed the guitar signal through an analogue distortion unit such as the Ibanez TS-9 Tube Screamer for a fuzzy rhythm sound. The resonant woody tones of the ES-335 guitars are evident throughout the track despite this treatment.

Fascinating fact:
The band are named after a motorcycle gang led by the actor Marlon Brando in the film *The Wild One* (1953).
The song 'Spread Your Love' bears a remarkable similarity to Norman Greenbaum's 'Spirit In The Sky' – this must be intentional, just listen to the short lead lick at the end of the intro!

Technical tips:
Don't waste time trying to play the exact same strum each time – it makes little difference if you hit four strings on the first chord and three on the next, just take the spirit of it and knock it out.

Note too that the open chords between each barre chord are simply the result of releasing the previous chord momentarily.

Most memorable lyric:
Spread your love like a fever
And don't you ever come down
Spread your love like a fever
And don't you ever come down
I spread my love like a fever
I ain't ever coming down.

© 1999 BRMC Music, USA
Warner/Chappell North America Ltd, London W6 8BS

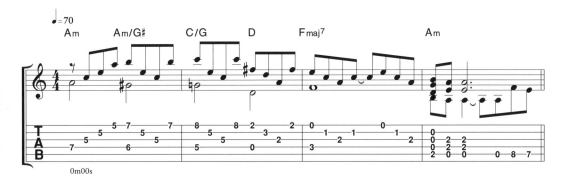

Words and music by:
Jimmy Page and Robert Plant

From the album:
Led Zeppelin IV (1971)

Guitarist:
Jimmy Page

Set-up:
1971 Martin D28 steel string acoustic guitar

Fascinating fact:
We've mentioned backwards messages earlier in this book (see page 76 – 'Money'). The king of the alleged 'back masking' songs is surely 'Stairway To Heaven'. According to popular legend, if the section of the song that runs from "If there's a bustle" through to "There's still time to change the road you're on", is played backwards it produces these lyrics:

Oh, here's to my sweet Satan
The one whose little path would make me sad
Whose power is Satan
He'll give you, give you 666
There was a little toolshed
Where he made us suffer
Sad Satan

Actually, it does sound vaguely similar! But are we really to believe that Robert and Jimmy suffered some terrible abuse by Satan? Where is this little toolshed anyway – surely it should have made its way onto an album cover or inner sleeve at the very least? And why did they choose such bad lyrics for their satanic devotional passage – wouldn't that just get them in even more trouble, maybe another trip to the little toolshed?!

You have been warned:
This transcription is printed for research purposes only. Novice readers, no doubt chuffed at nailing the riff, should avoid playing it in premises that sell guitars. Such behaviour results in abuse at best, and in the worst-case scenario forcible ejection from the premises. Ensuing legal action is likely to follow from the store manager. The same goes for 'Smoke On The Water' (see page 108). Curiously, with Ozzy Osbourne's return to mass popularity we can safely remove 'Paranoid' from the list of banned tunes.

Most memorable lyric:
If there's a bustle in your hedgerow
Don't be alarmed now
It's just a spring clean for the May queen
Yes there are two paths you can go by
But in the long run
There's still time to change the road you're on.

© 1972 Superhype Music Inc, USA
Warner/Chappell Music Ltd, London W6 8BS

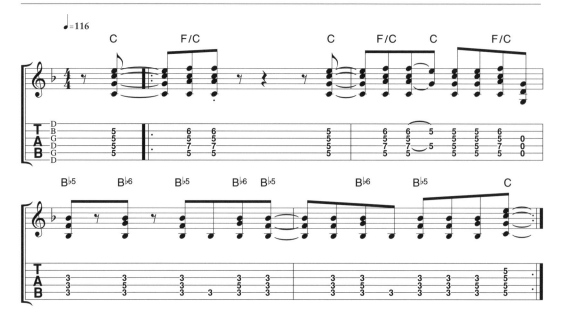

Words and music by:
Mick Jagger and Keith Richards

From the album:
Tattoo You (1981)

Highest chart placing (UK):
7 (1981)

Highest chart placing (US):
2 (1981)

Guitarist:
Keith Richards

Set-up:
Fender Telecaster through a Fender Twin

Fascinating fact:
Most bands at one time or another have stuff hurled at them on stage. Keith always takes extra care when playing in Germany, as he's had two famous incidents that he doesn't want to repeat – he slipped on a frankfurter in Frankfurt, and nearly fell off stage when he trod on a hamburger in Hamburg.

Most memorable lyric:
I've been running hot
You got me ticking gonna blow my top
If you start me up
If you start me up
I'll never stop
You make a grown man cry
You make a grown man cry
You make a grown man cry
Spread out the oil, the gasoline
I walk smooth,
Ride in a mean, mean machine.

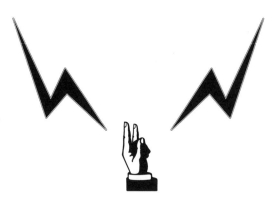

'Five strings, three chords, two fingers, one asshole.'
Keith Richards

© 1978 Promopub BV, Netherlands
EMI Music Publishing Ltd, London WC2H 0QY

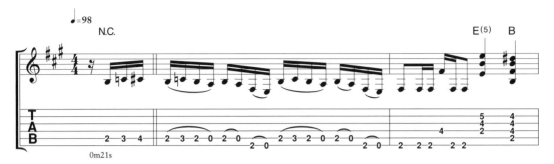

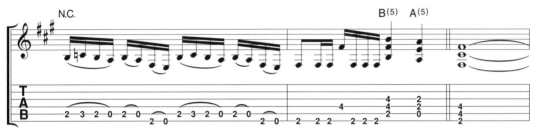

Words and music by:
David Coverdale and John Sykes

From the album:
Whitesnake (1987)

Highest chart placing (UK):
16 (1987)

Guitarist:
John Sykes

Set-up:
Gibson Les Paul Custom Mesa Boogie Coliseum heads and Marshall 4x12 cabs

How to get that sound:
John gets his distortion by overdriving the amp and letting the power amps work hard. You'll need to saturate the sound with distortion with a gain setting of around 9/10.

Be sure to check the sound of the chords and not just the single note line in the riff, especially the B chord. It's a major chord not a power chord, so too much distortion or bad tonal selection will transform it into a messy mixture of overtones and oscillating fuzz.

Obviously this is another showcase for the bridge pickup, the tone cetainly has the bite and attack of a high output humbucker.

Most memorable lyric:
In the still of the night
I hear the wolf howl, honey
Sniffing around your door
In the still of the night
I feel my heart beating heavy
Telling me I gotta have more.

In the shadow of night
I see the full moon rise
Telling me what's in store,
My heart start aching
My body start a-shaking
And I can't take no more, no, no, no.

S

© 1987 Whitesnake Music Ltd and Whitesnake Music (Overseas) Ltd, USA
Warner/Chappell Music Ltd, London W6 8BS

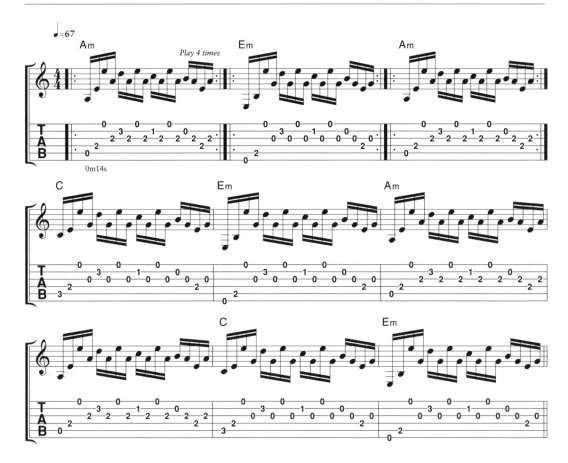

Words and music by:
Thomas Yorke, Edward O'Brien, Colin Greenwood, Jonathan Greenwood and Philip Selway

From the album:
The Bends (1994)

Highest chart placing (UK):
5 (1996)

Guitarist:
Johnny Greenwood

Set-up:
Fender Starcaster semi-acoustic guitar

Technical tips:
This is a great riff for getting alternate picking with string skipping going!

Most memorable lyric:
Rows of houses all bearing down on me
I can feel their blue hands touching me
All these things into position
All these things we'll one day swallow whole
And fade out again ...

© 1994 Warner/Chappell Music Ltd, London W6 8BS

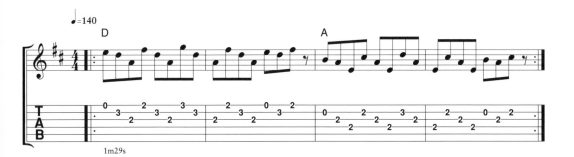

1m29s

Words and music by:
Bryan Adams and Jim Vallance

From the album:
Reckless (1984)

Highest chart placing (US):
5 (1985)

Guitarist:
Keith Scott

Set-up:
Gibson Les Paul through a Marshall stack

Fascinating fact:
Bryan once attended a concert by Deep Purple – that night Ritchie Blackmore pointed his guitar into the crowd and Bryan watched in amazement as a fan at the front of the crowd jumped up and grabbed Ritchie's guitar, pulling it straight from his hands and disappearing with it back into the crowd. The fan held onto it for a few moments before he was found by several security men and forced to give it up.
That fan turned out to be Keith Scott, unknown to Bryan at the time, who ultimately became the guitarist in Bryan's band.

Technical tips:
The best way to pick this is to use strict alternate picking – if you haven't tried this before with a chordal riff then this is a great place to start. It may seem odd at first, especially as the first time you play the top string you play a downstroke, and the next time you play it you use an upstroke. Stick with it and persevere, because once mastered it gives the smoothest result.

Most memorable lyric:
I got my first real six string
Bought it at the five and dime
Played it till my fingers bled
Was the summer of '69
Me and some guys from school had a band
And we tried real hard
Jimmy quit and Joey got married
Shoulda known we'd never get far
Oh when I look back now
That summer seemed to last forever
And if I had a choice, yeah
I'd always wanna be there
Those were the best days of my life.

© 1984 Adams Communications Inc and Testatyme Music, USA
Rondor Music (London) Ltd, London W6 8JA

Sunshine Of Your Love

Cream

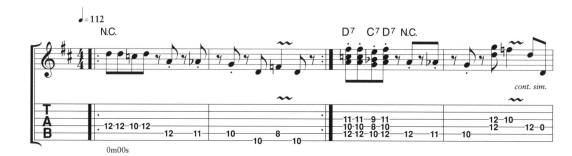

Words and music by:
Eric Clapton, Jack Bruce and Peter Brown

From the album:
Disraeli Gears (1967)

Highest chart placing (UK):
25 (1968)

Highest chart placing (US):
5 (1968)

Guitarist:
Eric Clapton

Set-up:
Gibson SG through a Marshall stack

How to get that sound:
This song showcases a sound that Eric called 'woman tone', which is achieved by setting the tone control of the neck pickup to zero. When overdriven the sound is very rich, with a deep clarinet-like timbre.

Fascinating fact:
Eric recorded this song with a Gibson SG that he bought to replace a stolen Les Paul. He had it painted by Seemon and Marijke Posthuma, a couple known on the London art scene as The Fool. The body depicts a winged cherub sitting on a cloud with the sun shining behind and surrounded by stars: beneath her feet a fire burns – presumably hell. The guitar was given to George Harrison (The Beatles), who gave it to Jackie Lomax (The Undertakers), who sold it in 1974 to Todd Rundgren (Utopia, Rundgren) for $500. Todd sold it for $150,000 in 2000.

Strange similarities:
Is it just my imagination or does Eric start the solo by playing 'Blue Moon'?

Most memorable lyric:
It's getting near dawn
When lights close their tired eyes
I'll soon be with you my love
To give you my dawn surprise
I'll be with you darling soon
I'll be with you when the stars start falling.

© 1968 E.C. Music Ltd and Dratleaf Ltd
E.C. Music Ltd, London W1D 3JB and Warner/Chappell Music Ltd, London W6 8BS

Words and music by:

Lindsey Buckingham, John McVie, Christine McVie, Mick Fleetwood and Stevie Nicks

From the album:

Rumours (1977)

Guitarist:

Lindsey Buckingham

Set-up:

National Resonator guitar

Technical tips:

Pan your hi-fi balance hard left to listen to the acoustic part in detail. This 'Travis Picking' style uses the first and index fingers on the top three strings, interjecting notes against an alternating bass line played by the thumb on the lower three strings. The famous bass line that enters at 3'05" is also included here for completeness.

Most memorable lyric:

And if you don't love me now
You will never love me again
I can still hear you saying
You would never break the chain.

© 1976 Now Sounds Music, New Entertainment Music, Molly Mac Music, Rattleman Music and Welsh Witch Music, USA. Warner/Chappell Music Ltd, London W6 8BS, EMI Music Publishing Ltd, London WC2H 0QY, BMG Music Publishing Ltd, London SW6 3JW and Sony/ATV Music Publishing, London W1V 2LP

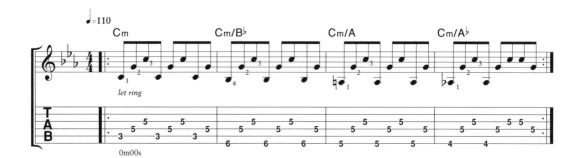

Words and music by:
Paul Weller and Brendan Lynch

From the album:
Stanley Road (1995)

Highest chart placing (UK):
7 (1995)

Guitarist:
Paul Weller

Set-up:
Epiphone Casino through a Marshall Bluesbreaker 2x12 combo

How to get that sound:
The Epiphone Casino is a semi-acoustic guitar fitted with single coil P90 pickups; it has a warm woody tone and noticeable bite in the top end. Plugging such an instrument direct into a vintage valve combo set for mild overdrive produces the distinctive hollow bass notes and jangly highs that characterise 'The Changingman'. The Casino was a favourite guitar of John Lennon, and features on several Smiths tracks in the capable hands of Johnny Marr. All the more reason to buy one – buying a semi is the only way to get that sound!

Technical tips:
Follow the finger numbering very carefully if you want to avoid fingerboard acrobatics – it's actually pretty straightforward. There are some valid alternatives that you should also try – the riff sounds great in the open position (although it's a little harder to play there for some), plus you may find that ditching the pick in favour of playing fingerstyle suits you better.

Most memorable lyric:
I'm the changingman
Built on shifting sands
I'm the changingman
Waiting for the bang
As I light a bitter fuse.

T

© 1995 Solid Bond Productions Ltd and Notting Hill Music (UK) Ltd
BMG Music Publishing Ltd, London SW6 3JW and Notting Hill Music (UK) Ltd, London W8 4AP

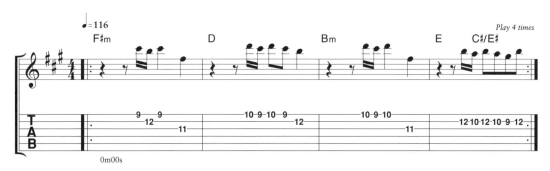

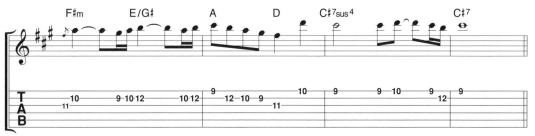

Words and music by:
Joey Tempest

From the album:
The Final Countdown (1986)

Highest chart placing (UK):
1 (1986)

Highest chart placing (US):
8 (1987)

Guitarist:
John Norum

Keyboards:
Mic Michaeli

How to get that sound:
Here we've transcribed the famous keyboard intro – if you're not fussy about authenticity just bang it out with lots of distortion, alternatively this could be your introduction to MIDI guitar!
The Roland GK-2A and Shadow SH075 MIDI pickups are very popular designs and can both be retrofitted to most guitars. They're far thinner than regular pickups and are usually fitted between the bridge pickup and the bridge. A cable connects the pickup to a small unit that's attached to the scratchplate (or behind the bridge) which is used to control volume and patch changes.

Attach a MIDI cable to the control unit and then plug into the synth or sampler of your choice and you have access to an enormous tonal palette limited only by your (or your dad's) wallet.

Most memorable lyric:
We're heading for Venus
And still we stand tall
'Cause maybe they've seen us
And welcome us all, yeah
With so many light years to go
And things to be found
I'm sure that we'll all miss her so
It's the final countdown.

© 1986 EMI Music Publishing Ltd, London WC2H 0QY

The Power Of Love

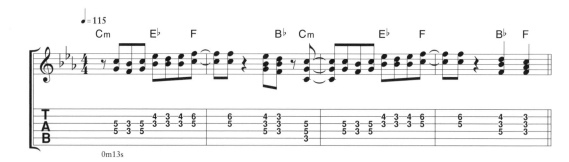

Words and music by:
Chris Hayes, Huey Lewis and John Colla

From the album:
Back To The Future (Soundtrack) (1985)

Highest chart placing (UK):
9 (1986)

Highest chart placing (US):
1 (1985)

Guitarist:
Chris Hayes

Set-up:
Fender Stratocaster

How to get that sound:
Put the pickup toggle switch in the middle position and add plenty of compression. The sound is very clean, so The News may very well have used what's called a DI or Direct Inject – in other words, plugging the guitar directly into the desk via a DI box. The DI box is a small transformer that matches the guitar output signal to a level that can be used by the mixing desk.

Technical tips:
Playing two-note chords (or *diads*) is known as double stopping. Make sure you use partial barre chords wherever notes are at the same fret and try to play the riff as though it's a melody rather than a series of chord changes.
When you get to a rest, use the side of your palm to damp the strings near the bridge. Don't do anything fancy with the pick, just use all downstrokes.

Most memorable lyric:
The power of love is a curious thing
Make a one man weep, make another man sing
Change a hawk to a little white dove
More than a feeling
That's the power of love.

Tougher than diamonds, rich like cream
Stronger and harder than a bad girl's dream
Make a bad one good make a wrong one right
Power of love that keeps you home at night.

You don't need money
Don't take fame
Don't need no credit card
To ride this train
It's strong and it's sudden
And it's cruel sometimes
But it might just save your life
That's the power of love
That's the power of love.

© 1985 Kinda Blue Music, Huey Lewis Music and Cause & Effect Music, USA
Warner/Chappell North America Ltd, London W6 8BS

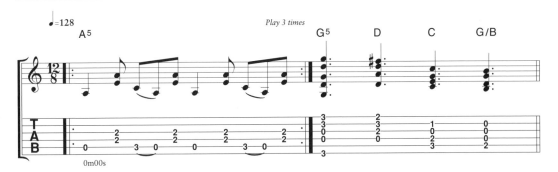

Words and music by:
Brian May

From the album:
A Day At The Races (1976)

Highest chart placing (UK):
31 (1977)

Highest chart placing (US):
49 (1977)

Guitarist:
Brian May

Set-up:
Self made guitar and Vox AC30 amplifiers

How to get that sound:
This is Brian's guitar set for straight ahead rock – bridge pickup, all the controls open, and plenty of gain at the amp. He's probably also using his treble booster to drive the tubes in his AC30 a little harder.
Aim to use real (or modelled) classic British tube distortion – these amps will probably have low gain by modern standards, so a gain setting of 9/10 or 10/10 will probably be needed.
(See also page 13 – 'Another One Bites The Dust', page 25 – 'Bohemian Rhapsody' and page 38 – 'Fat Bottomed Girls')

Fascinating fact:
In the studio Brian often uses 'Deacy', an amplifier named after Queen bassist John Deacon who constructed it. It's basically an amplifier from a car radio combined with a small hi-fi speaker, which outputs barely a single watt of power.

Technical tips:
Don't be put off by the 12/8 time signature, it's just like 4/4 but each beat has a triplet feel.
Confused? Here's the low-down on what's going on. Firstly, think of a steady pulse of four beats:

1   2   3   4

... next, add a triple feel to each beat by counting "two - three" after each beat.

1 *2 3* 2 *2 3* 3 *2 3* 4 *2 3*

Most memorable lyric:
Get your party gown
And get your pigtail down
And get your heart beatin' baby
Got my timin' right
And got my act all tight
It's gotta be tonight
My little school babe
Your momma says you don't
And your daddy says you won't
And I'm boilin' up inside
Ain't no way I'm gonna lose out this time.

© 1976 Queen Music Ltd, London WC2H 0QY

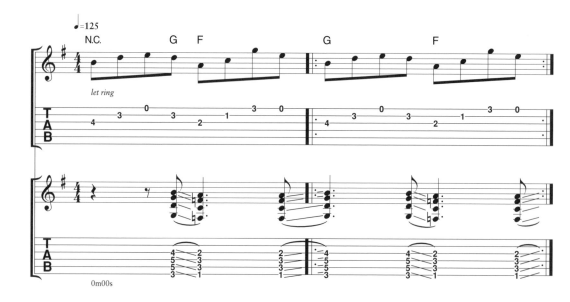

Words and music by:
Raymond Davies

From the album:
Kinda Kinks (1965)

Highest chart placing (UK):
1 (1965)

Highest chart placing (US):
6 (1965)

Guitarist:
Ray Davies
Dave Davies

Set-up:
Fender Telecaster and Harmony Meteor
(See also page 11 – 'All Day & All Of The Night')

Most memorable lyric:
I'm so tired
Tired of waiting
Tired of waiting for you
I'm so tired
Tired of waiting
Tired of waiting for you
I was a lonely soul
I had nobody till I met you
But you keep me waiting
All of the time
What can I do?

Technical tips:
This song features Ray's carefully picked arpeggio line with Dave's pre-punk driving rhythm. The brothers endured a highly charged sibling rivalry that occasionally got out of hand. Once, in a restaurant, Ray stabbed Dave in the chest with his fork for stealing a french fry. More recently they released autobigraphies at almost the same time, Ray's *X-Ray* was described as 'flowery' by Dave, whose own effort *Kink* is painfully honest and open by comparison.

© 1964 Edward Kassner Music Co Ltd, London SW6 6SE

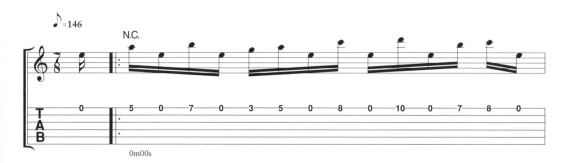

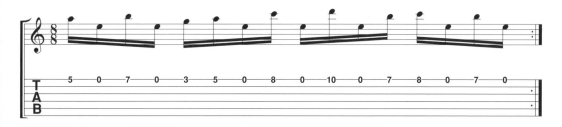

Music by:
Mike Oldfield

From the album:
Tubular Bells (1973)

Highest chart placing (UK):
31 (1974)

Highest chart placing (US):
7 (1974)

Electric Guitars, Acoustic Guitars, Spanish Guitar, Bass Guitars, Fuzz Guitars, Speed Elec. Guitars, Guitars sounding like Bagpipes, Mandolin-like Guitar, Grand Piano, Honky Tonk, Taped motor drive amplifier organ chord, Lowrey Organ, Farfisa Organ, Hammond Organ, Piltdown Man, Moribund Chorus, Flageolet, Assorted Percussion, Glockenspiel, Concert Tympani and Tubular Bells:
Mike Oldfield

Set-up:
Piano arranged for guitar

Most memorable lyric:
Two slightly distorted guitars!

Fascinating fact:
'Tubular Bells' was one of the pieces selected to try and convince the general public of the merits of quadrophonic sound.

In 1975 a double album named *Quadfile* was released. Each of the four sides contained the same tracks, including two sections from 'Tubular Bells', 'Money' by Pink Floyd from *Dark Side Of The Moon*, classical recordings of Mahler and Bartók scores and some light jazz from Yehudi Menuhin and Stephane Grappelli.

Where video had the competing systems of VHS and Betamax, there were (of course!) four systems competing for the quadrophonic market. As a result, the four identical sides on *Quadfile* had one essential difference, each was mastered in one of the quadrophonic technologies – CD-4, QS, UD-4 and SQ.

There were serious logistical problems in making *Quadfile* – the producers had to get all the artists' consent and the agreement of the manufacturers CBS (SQ), JVC (CD-4), Nippon Columbia (UD-4) and Sansui (QS). Furthermore, each of the manufacturers had to receive identical four track master tapes from which to prepare their demonstration.

When the project finally went to press the public had already become jaded by the lack of a clear market leader and interest in quadrophony was in serious recession. *Quadfile* was limited to a single run of 5,000 pressings and is now a sought-after collectors item.

It would be another 20 years before surround sound became a viable option in the home, driven by interest in film rather than music.

© 1973 EMI Virgin Music Ltd, London WC2H 0QY

0m42s
Tune down a semitone to match key of original recording

Words and music by:
Ian Dench, James Atkin, Zachary Foley, Mark DeCloedt and Derran Brownson

From the album:
Schubert Dip (1990)

Highest chart placing (UK):
3 (1990)

Highest chart placing (US):
1 (1991)

Guitarist:
Ian Dench

How to get that sound:
Use an analogue distortion pedal set for a fairly high clip. As with most rock single note guitar lines, use the guitar's bridge pickup with the volume and tone controls left wide open. Shape the tone with some emphasis on the mid and high frequencies. Add a little compression and reverb.

Curious Covers:
Tom Jones covered this as a B-side to his version of Talking Heads' 'Burning Down The House'.

Fascinating fact:
There is some uncertainty over the exact origin of EMF's name. It stands for either *Epsom Mad Funkers* or *Ecstasy Mother F***ers* depending on which interview you read.

Technical tips:
This is a great riff for novices and will get all your fretting hand fingers involved. Use the 'one finger per fret' rule – first finger at the 5th fret, second finger at the 6th fret, third finger at the 7th fret and little finger at the 8th fret.

To be in tune with the original recording you'll need to tune all your strings down a semitone (the same distance as one fret on the guitar). The easiest way for novices to do this is with the aid of a chromatic guitar tuner. You would then use the tuner to tune the strings to (low thick string to high skinny string):

$$E\flat \quad A\flat \quad D\flat \quad G\flat \quad B\flat \quad E\flat$$

Ordinary guitar tuners will only allow you to tune in standard tuning – E A D G B E.

Most memorable lyric:
You burden me with your questions
You'd have me tell no lies
You're always asking what it's all about
Now listen to my replies
You say to me I don't talk enough
But when I do I'm a fool
These times I've spent, I've realized
I'm going to shoot through
And leave you.

© 1990 Warner/Chappell Music Ltd, London W6 8BS

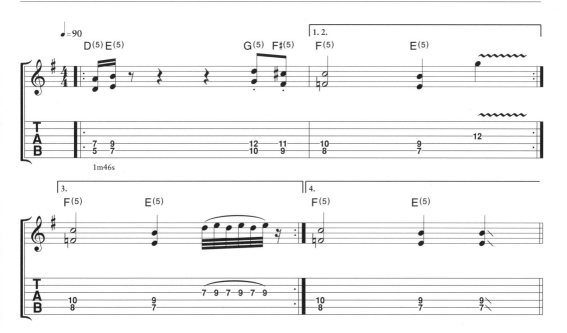

Words and music by:
John Osbourne, William Ward, Terence Butler and Frank Iommi

From the album:
Paranoid (1970)

Guitarist:
Tony Iommi

Set-up:
Gibson SG through a Laney stack

How to get that sound:
See page 56 ('Iron Man') and page 83 ('Paranoid')

Fascinating fact:
When Ozzy met George Bush, the President told him "My mother loves your stuff".

Magnificent Merchandise:
Following the success of MTV's 'reality sitcom' show, *The Osbournes*, McFarlane produced an Ozzy action figure clad in leather wielding a crucifix. Ozzy dolls were also manufactured, some had voice chips which, when activated uttered phrases such as "Sharrrrrrrron!" or "I'm the Prince of f***ing Darkness!".

Most memorable lyric:
Generals gathered in their masses
Just like witches at black masses
Evil minds that plot destruction
Sorcerers of death's construction
In the fields the bodies burning
As the war machine keeps turning
Death and hatred to mankind
Poisoning their brainwashed minds
Oh lord, yeah!

W

© 1970 Westminster Music Ltd, London SW10 0SZ

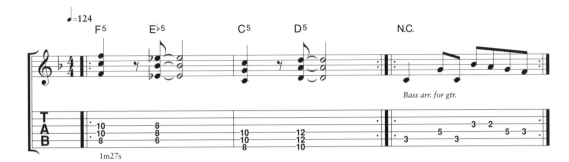

Words and music by:
Barry Mann and Cynthia Weil

From the album:
Animal Tracks (1965) US Release

Highest chart placing (UK):
2 (1965)

Highest chart placing (US):
13 (1965)

Guitarist:
Hilton Valentine

Set-up:
Gretsch Tennessean through a Vox AC30

How to get that sound:
There's quite a lot of bright attack on the guitar. Use a semi-acoustic with the bridge pickup selected and the volume and tone controls fully open. With a vintage valve amp (or an AC30 setting on an amp modelling preamp) set the gain as high as you can without the signal clipping. Reduce the bass and push the mid and high frequencies with the tone controls.

Fascinating fact:
Keyboardist Alan Price left The Animals in 1966 at the height of their popularity. He had a fear of flying and could not maintain the band's international commitments.
Hilton Valentine was quite a wild man by 60s standards, he'd spice up shows by ripping off his shirt or spinning around on his back. He left the group in 1965 and was succeeded by a number of guitarists including Andy Summers (The Police).

Most memorable lyric:
In this dirty old part of the city
Where the sun refused to shine
People tell me
There ain't no use in tryin'.

Now my girl you're so young and pretty
And one thing I know is true
You'll be dead
Before your time is due
I know.

We gotta get out of this place
If it's the last thing we ever do
We gotta get out of this place
'Cause girl, there's a better life
For me and you.

© 1965 Screen Gems-EMI Music Inc, USA
Screen Gems-EMI Music Ltd, London WC2H 0QY

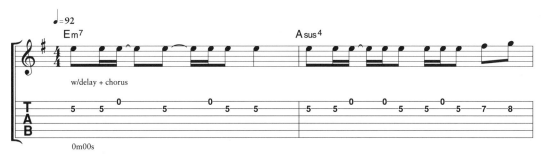

Words and music by:
Neil Finn and Tim Finn

From the album:
Woodface (1991)

Highest chart placing (UK):
7 (1992)

Guitarist:
Tim Finn

Set-up:
1968 Gibson Les Paul Goldtop through a Vox AC30

How to get that sound:
Select your guitar's rhythm (neck) pickup. If you don't own a vintage British amp but you have an amp modelling preamp head straight for the Vox AC30 patch. Even on a clean sound like this it's worth using the tonal colours and cabinet emulation that such units provide.
The sound is very clean – set the gain to no higher than 3/10. Add some echo with a delay of about 500ms and the mix set to 60% – this will ensure the effect is heard clearly without allowing it to take over and swamp the direct signal. Likewise, allow the repeats to fade quite fast – one repeat followed by a more distant second repeat will suffice. Add a little reverb and then shape the tone at the amp to keep the sound warm but bright.

Most memorable lyric:
Things ain't cooking in my kitchen
Strange afflictions wash over me
Julius Caesar and the Roman Empire
Couldn't conquer the blue sky.

© 1991 Roundhead Music and Rebel Larynx Music, USA
EMI Music Publishing Ltd, London WC2H 0QY

What Difference Does It Make?

The Smiths

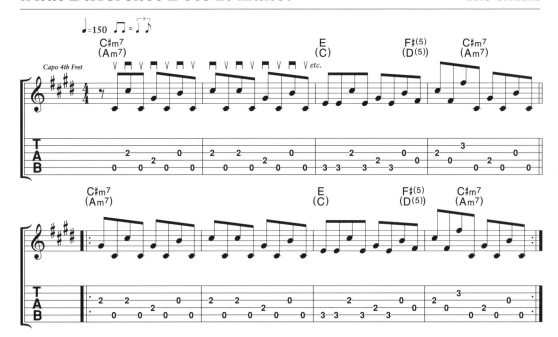

Words and music by:
Johnny Marr and Stephen Morrissey

From the album:
The Smiths (1984)

Highest chart placing (UK):
12 (1984)

Guitarist:
Johnny Marr

Set-up:
Fender Telecaster through a Roland Jazz Chorus

How to get that sound:
Johnny didn't like the guitar sound on The Smiths at all, and knew exactly where to lay the blame – "Overall, what I really didn't like about the records then was the amp, the Roland Jazz Chorus – that's the f***in' prime suspect".

The Jazz Chorus sounds great when you're there standing right next to it, but it's notoriously difficult to capture the sound in the recording studio. Close miking each speaker and then replaying the result through monitors 20 feet apart or through headphones just doesn't produce the same result.

(See also page 100 – 'She Sells Sanctuary')

Most memorable lyric:
All men have secrets and here is mine
So let it be known
For we have been through hell and high tide
I can surely rely on you
And yet you start to recoil
Heavy words are so lightly thrown
But still I'd leap in front of a
Flying bullet for you.

© 1984 Marr Songs Ltd and Bona Relations Ltd
Warner/Chappell Music Ltd, London W6 8BS and Copyright Control

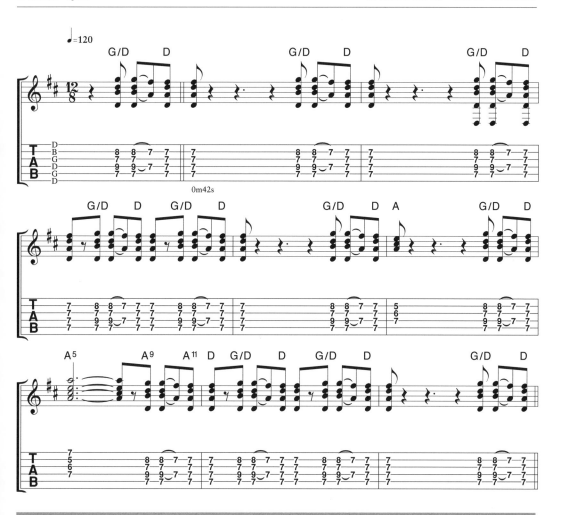

Words and music by:
Richard Parfitt and Andy Bown

From the album:
Whatever You Want (1979)

Highest chart placing (UK):
4 (1979)

Guitarists:
The Gomorr
The Womorr
(See page 35 – 'Down Down')

Set-up:
Fender Telecaster through a Vox AC30

Fascinating fact:
In 1999 Status Quo embarked on a tour of pubs to promote their album *Under The Influence*. Competitions run in newspapers *The Sun* (UK) and *Das Bild* (Germany) asked readers to nominate pubs for the band to perform in. Lucky winners included *The Spinners Arms* in Wigan. Earlier in the year they played to a crowd of 35,000 on the same bill as Michael Jackson.

Most memorable lyric:
Whatever you want
Whatever you like
Whatever you say
You pay your money
You take your choice
Whatever you need
Whatever you use
Whatever you win
Whatever you lose.

© 1979 EMI Music Publishing Ltd, London WC2H 0QY

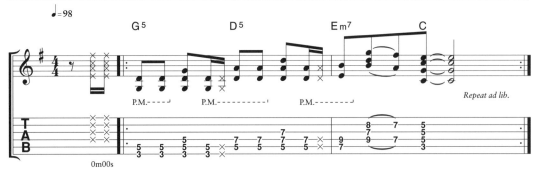

Tune guitar down a semitone to match key of original recording

---

Words and music by:
Billy Armstrong, Frank Wright and Michael Pritchard

From the album:
Dookie (1994)

Highest chart placing (UK):
27 (1995)

Guitarist:
Billie Joe Armstrong

Set-up:
Fernandes Stratocaster copy through a Marshall Stack

How to get that sound:
The guitar sound on this track is nearly identical to that of 'Basketcase' (see page 16). For the first two bars the riff is played on one guitar panned hard left, and is then doubled in bar three by another guitar panned hard right.

Fascinating fact:
'Blue', Billie Joe's Fernandes Stratocaster copy, which was used all over Dookie, has been retired of late in favour a gaggle of new instruments that include a Gibson Les Paul, a Gibson ES-175 and various customised Fender Telecasters.
The Fernandes has been refretted so many times that there's barely enough wood for new frets to be attached to.

Technical tips:
By playing the opening power chords with your first and third fingers you can set up the D♯m7 chord in bar three before you get there.

Most memorable lyric:
I heard it all before
So don't knock down my door
I'm a loser and a user
So I don't need no accuser
To try and slag me down
Because I know you're right.

So go do what you like
Make sure you do it wise
You may find out that your self-doubt
Means nothing was ever there
You can't go forcing something
If it's just not right.

© 1994 Green Daze Music, USA
Warner/Chappell North America Ltd, London W6 8BS

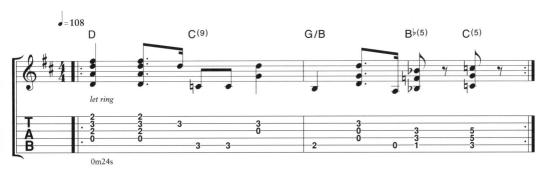

Words and music by:
Peter Brown and Jack Bruce

Most memorable lyric:
*At the party
She was kindness
In the hard crowd
Consolation
For the old wound
Now forgotten
Yellow tigers
Crouched in jungles
In her dark eyes
She's just dressing
Goodbye windows
Tired starlings.*

From the album:
Wheels Of Fire (1968)

Highest chart placing (UK):
28 (1969)

Highest chart placing (US):
6 (1968)

Guitarist:
Eric Clapton

Set-up:
Gibson SG through a Marshall stack

How to get that sound:
Use a guitar with a humbucker in the bridge position and feed it into either a fuzz box or direct into an amp set for mild crunchy distortion. Note that there's no reverb on the original recording.

Fascinating fact:
There's a persistent apocryphal story that tells of a vicar named Father Dennis Ackroyd, who visited a large house while making the rounds in his local parish of Ewhurst. While chatting to the home owner, who introduced himself only as Eric, Father Dennis noticed a guitar in the room and suggested that Eric play at the church one day. Eric readily agreed and Father Dennis said "Good! I'll give you a couple of months to practice." Apparently Eric played at several children's services in the tiny Surrey church, performing *Amazing Grace* among other hymns, much to the delight of the congregation.

W

© 1976 Dratleaf Ltd
Warner/Chappell Music Ltd, London W6 8BS

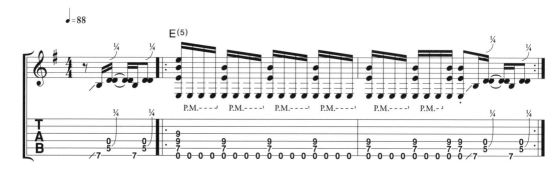

Words and music by:
Jimmy Page, Robert Plant, John Bonham, John Paul Jones and Willie Dixon

From the album:
Led Zeppelin II (1969)

Highest chart placing (UK):
21 (1997)

Guitarist:
Jimmy Page

Set-up:
Gibson Les Paul through a Marshall Stack

How to get that sound:
This is another outing for Jimmy's custom made Roger Mayer fuzz box. Use the bridge pickup and leave all the controls wide open, adding plenty of high E.Q. at the amp.
The original recording has the guitar panned hard left with most of the reverb panned hard right – this is probably just overspill in the vocal mic, with Jimmy absolutely belting it out in another room.

Fascinating fact:
There are numerous scandalous rumours about Led Zeppelin band members. On one occasion Jimmy Page was allegedly covered in whipped cream, placed on a room service trolley and wheeled into a roomful of young female fans.
The most disturbing story however, tells of the band pleasuring a female groupie with a live shark. There are many variations of this tale, but one detail was cleared up by Richard Cole, the band's manager: "But the true shark story was that it wasn't even a shark. It was a red snapper".

Most memorable lyric:
You've been coolin'
Baby I've been droolin'
All the good times
I've been misusin'
Way, way down inside
I'm gonna give you my love
I'm gonna give you every inch of my love
Gonna give you my love
Yeah!
All right!
Let's go!

© 1970 Flames Of Albion Music Inc, USA
Warner/Chappell Music Ltd, London W6 8BS

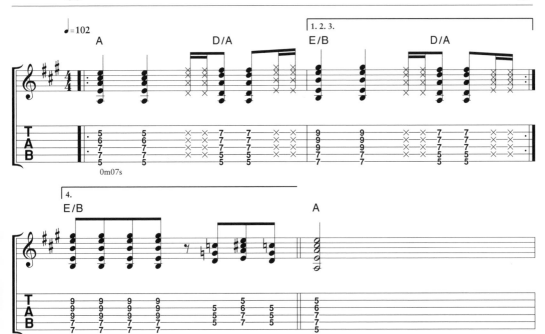

Words and music by:
Chip Taylor

From the album:
Wild Thing (1966)

Highest chart placing (UK):
2 (1966)

Highest chart placing (US):
1 (1966)

Guitarist:
Chris Britton

Set-up:
Burns Double-Six

Fascinating fact:
Reg Presley, The Troggs lead singer, is a devoted researcher of UFOs, crop circles, monatomic gold, alchemy and other unexplained phenomenon. In his book *Wild Things They Don't Tell Us*, Reg expands on his theory that the Earth is slowly but surely changing shape, and argues that aliens have been among us for many years, and that governments have been going to extraordinary lengths to suppress the truth.

Most memorable lyric:
Wild thing
You make my heart sing
You make everything
Groovy
Wild thing!

Wild thing
I think I love you
But I wanna know for sure
So come on
Hold me tight
I love you ...

© 1966 EMI Blackwood Music Inc, USA
EMI Songs Ltd, London WC2H 0QY

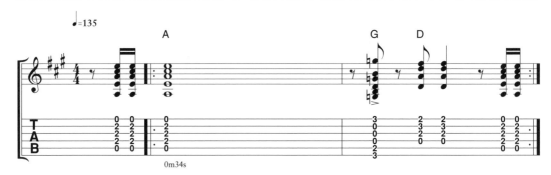

0m34s

Words and music by:
Peter Townshend

From the album:
Who's Next (1971)

Highest chart placing (UK):
9 (1971)

Highest chart placing (US):
15 (1971)

Guitarist:
Pete Townshend

Set-up:
Gretsch Country Gentleman through a Fender Bandmaster amplifier via an Edwards pedal steel volume pedal

Dream setup:
Pete was given the Gretsch/Fender/Edwards setup by Joe Walsh (The Eagles). Pete had given Joe an ARP 2600 synthesizer, and Joe returned the favour by giving Pete a replica of the equipment setup used by Neil Young.
Pete thought the orange Gretsch looked ugly, and wasn't expecting much when he plugged it in, but was taken aback by the sound and described it as " ... a sound from paradise".

Fascinating fact:
Pete is well known for smashing up his guitars on stage. Most of the time they were simply stock instruments that were very easily replaced, but in 1973 on *Top Of The Pops* he smashed up the beautiful orange Gretsch Country Gentleman that had been given to him by Joe Walsh.

Most memorable lyric:
I'll tip my hat to the new constitution
Take a bow for the new revolution
Smile and grin at the change all around
Pick up my guitar and play
Just like yesterday
Then I'll get on my knees and pray
We don't get fooled again
No, no!

"I played the guitar for ten years before I realised it wasn't a weapon."
Pete Townshend

© 1971 Fabulous Music Ltd, London SW10 0SZ

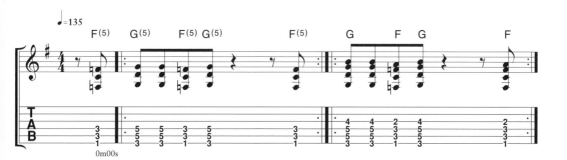

Words and music by:
Raymond Davies

From the album:
The Kinks (1964)

Highest chart placing (UK):
1 (1964)

Highest chart placing (US):
7 (1964)

Guitarist:
Dave Davies

Set-up:
Harmony Meteor through a 'customised' Elpico amplifier

How to get that sound:
To emulate this sound try using a semi-acoustic through a fuzz box, and then boost the high frequencies at the amp, at the same time reducing the bottom end.
(See also page 11 – 'All Day & All Of The Night')

Banned:
Just as The Kinks concluded their 1965 American tour, the American Federation of Musicians had them banned from re-entering the U.S. for five years. Various reasons were cited, including 'unprofessional conduct', but an alternative theory states that the Federation were unhappy at the growing number of British musicians invading the States and leaving with US dollars. The Kinks were singled out because their management and resources were not as powerful as those of The Beatles or The Rolling Stones.

Most memorable lyric:
Girl, you really got me goin'
You got me so I don't know what I'm doin'
Yeah, you really got me now
You got me so I can't sleep at night.

Yeah, you really got me now
You got me so I don't know what I'm doin', now
Oh yeah, you really got me now
You got me so I can't sleep at night.

You really got me
You really got me
You really got me.

© 1964 Edward Kassner Music Co Ltd, London SW6 6SE

Words and music by:
David Bowie

From the album:
The Rise And Fall Of Ziggy Stardust And The Spiders From Mars (1972)

Guitarist:
Mick Ronson

Set-up:
1968 Gibson Les Paul Custom through a Marshall stack

How to get that sound:
Here again we can hear Mick using his favourite 'fixed wah' trick. Mick would activate the wah-wah pedal and then experiment with pedal placement to find a fixed position at which he liked the sound. Used this way the wah pedal becomes a type of low tech parametric E.Q.

There are many different makes of wah-wah available today, and the design that Mick used is still available – the 'Cry Baby' Wah-Wah.

Another interesting feature of this track is the double tracking (recording the same guitar part twice). The riff we've transcribed is the guitar panned hard right in the mix – the other guitar, panned hard left is the same for the first bar, but plays ringing chords in the next.

Double tracking is used to thicken up the guitar sounds – it's impossible to *exactly* replicate a performance, and the miniscule differences add an almost chorus-like effect to a part.

Many producers keep the tracked parts identical, but tracking also offers the possibility of adding a wider harmonic pallette to the song by, for example, stacking up chord voicings or adding harmonies.

(See also page 91 – 'Rebel Rebel')

Fascinating fact:
Mick was a busy session player and contributed many riffs and guitar parts to projects without ever getting a writing credit, such as on *Jack And Diane* by John Mellencamp.

Most memorable lyric:
Ziggy played guitar
Jamming good with weird and Gilly
The spiders from Mars
He played it left hand
But made it too far
Became the special man
Then we were Ziggy's band.

© 1971 EMI Music Publishing Ltd, Moth Music and Tintoretto Music
EMI Music Publishing Ltd, London WC2H 0QY, Chrysalis Music Ltd, London W10 6SP and RZO Music Ltd, London W1M 5FF

Songs guitars were meant to play

Essential Acoustic Playlist 2
9854A   VC   ISBN: 1-84328-411-1

A Minha Meninha (The Bees) – Ain't That Enough (Teenage Fanclub) – All Together Now (The Farm) – Alright (Supergrass) – Am I Wrong (Mull Historical Society) – American English (Idlewild) – Average Man (Turin Brakes) – Beetlebum (Blur) – Breakfast at Tiffany's (Deep Blue Something) – Buy It In Bottles (Richard Ashcroft) – Can You Dig It? (The Mock Turtles) – Caught By The River (Doves) – Coffee & TV (Blur) – Come Away With Me (Norah Jones) – Come Back To What You Know (Embrace) – Common People (Pulp) – Crazy Beat (Blur) – Creep (Radiohead) – A Design For Life (Manic Street Preachers) – Distant Sun (Crowded House) – Don't Let Me Down Gently (The Wonderstuff) – Don't Think You're The First (The Coral) – Everlong (Foo Fighters) – Fallen Angel (Elbow) – Fastboy (The Bluetones) – The Final Arrears (Mull Historical Society) – Forget About Tomorrow (Feeder) – Getting Away With It (Electronic) – Go To Sleep (Radiohead) – Grace (Supergrass) – Here's Where The Story Ends (The Sundays) – High And Dry (Radiohead) – History (The Verve) – Hooligan (Embrace) – I Need Direction (Teenage Fanclub) – I Will (Radiohead) – (I'm Gonna) Cry Myself Blind (Primal Scream) – In A Room (Dodgy) – It's True That We Love One Another (The White Stripes) – Just When You're Thinkin' Things Over (The Charlatans) – La Breeze (Simian) – Lilac Wine (Jeff Buckley) – A Little Like You (Grand Drive) – Live In A Hiding Place (Idlewild) – Lucky (Radiohead) – A Man Needs To Be Told (The Charlatans) – No Surprises (Radiohead) – Only Happy When It Rains (Garbage) – Out Of Time (Blur) – Painkiller (Turin Brakes) – Pass It On (The Coral) – Personal Jesus (Johnny Cash) – Pineapple Head (Crowded House) – Poor Misguided Fool (Starsailor) – Road Rage (Catatonia) – Seen The Light (Supergrass) – Seven Nation Army (The White Stripes) – Shine On (The House Of Love) – Silence Is Easy (Starsailor) – Sk8ter Boi (Avril Lavigne) – Stay Away From Me (The Star Spangles) – There There (Radiohead) – Thinking About Tomorrow (Beth Orton) – This Is How It Feels (Inspiral Carpets) – Wake Up Boo! (The Boo Radleys) – Words (Doves) – Yoshimi Battles The Pink Robots (Flaming Lips) – You're So Pretty – We're So Pretty (The Charlatans) – You've Got Her In Your Pocket (The White Stripes)

Essential Acoustic Playlist
9701A   VC   ISBN: 1-84328-207-0

All The Small Things (Blink 182) – All You Good Good People (Embrace) – Angie (The Rolling Stones) – Any Day Now (Elbow) – Bittersweet Symphony (The Verve) – Buddy (Lemonheads) – Burning Down The House (Talking Heads) – Central Reservation (Beth Orton) – Come Together (Primal Scream) – Cryin' (Aerosmith) – Don't Dream It's Over (Crowded House) – The Drugs Don't Work (The Verve) – Empty At The End (Electric Soft Parade) – Everybody Hurts (R.E.M.) – Everyday Is Like Sunday (Morrissey) – Fast Car (Tracey Chapman) – Fat Lip (Sum 41) – Fell In Love With A Girl (The White Stripes) – Fireworks (Embrace) – Fly Away (Lenny Kravitz) – Future Boy (Turin Brakes) – Going Places (Teenage Fanclub) – Good Riddance (Green Day) – Heaven Knows I'm Miserable Now (The Smiths) – Hotel California (The Eagles) – Hotel Yorba (The White Stripes) – Hunter (Dido) – It's A Shame About Ray (Lemonheads) – Karma Police (Radiohead) – Kiss Me (Sixpence None The Richer) – Losing My Religion (R.E.M.) – Love Burns (Black Rebel Motorcycle Club) – The Man Who Told Everything (Doves) – Mansize Rooster (Supergrass) – Mellow Doubt (Teenage Fanclub) – Movin' On Up (Primal Scream) – Moving (Supergrass) – Mr. Jones (Counting Crows) – Next Year (Foo Fighters) – Novocaine For The Soul (Eels) – Over The Rainbow (Eva Cassidy) – Panic (The Smiths) – Porcelain (Moby) – Pounding (Doves) – Powder Blue (Elbow) – Rhythm & Blues Alibi (Gomez) – Save Tonight (Eagle Eye Cherry) – Silent Sigh (Badly Drawn Boy) – Secret Smile (Semisonic) – Shot Shot (Gomez) – Silent To The Dark (Electric Soft Parade) – Slight Return (The Bluetones) – Soak Up The Sun (Sheryl Crow) – Something In My Eye (Ed Harcourt) – Something To Talk About (Badly Drawn Boy) – Song 2 (Blur) – Song For The Lovers (Richard Ashcroft) – Standing Still (Jewel) – Street Spirit (Fade Out) (Radiohead) – Teenage Dirtbag (Wheatus) – Tender (Blur) – There Goes The Fear (Doves) – Time In A Bottle (Jim Croce) – Underdog (Save Me) (Turin Brakes) – Walking After You (Foo Fighters) – Warning (Green Day) – Waterloo Sunset (The Kinks) – Weather With You (Crowded House) – Wicked Game (Chris Isaak) – Wild Wood (Paul Weller)

Classic Acoustic Playlist
9806A   VC   ISBN: 1-84328-332-8

Ain't No Sunshine (Bill Withers) – All Tomorrow's Parties (The Velvet Underground) – Alone Again Or (Love) – Another Brick In The Wall Part II (Pink Floyd) – Bad Moon Rising (Creedence Clearwater Revival) – Black Magic Woman (Fleetwood Mac) – Both Sides Now (Joni Mitchell) – Brain Damage/Eclipse (Pink Floyd) – Break On Through (The Doors) – California Dreamin' (The Mamas & The Papas) – Cocaine (Eric Clapton) – Cosmic Dancer (T. Rex) – Crazy Little Thing Called Love (Queen) – Daydream Believer (The Monkees) – Days (The Kinks) – Desperado (The Eagles) – Eight Miles High (The Byrds) – Everybody's Talkin' (Harry Nilsson) – Five Years (David Bowie) – For What It's Worth (Buffalo Springfield) – Fortunate Son (Creedence Clearwater Revival) – Get It On (T. Rex) – Handbags & Gladrags (Rod Stewart) – Happy (The Rolling Stones) – He Ain't Heavy, He's My Brother (The Hollies) – Heroin (The Velvet Underground) – A Horse With No Name (America) – I Feel The Earth Move (Carole King) – It's Only Rock And Roll (The Rolling Stones) – It's Too Late (Carole King) – Itchycoo Park (The Small Faces) – Layla (Eric Clapton) – Leaving On A Jet Plane (John Denver) – Life On Mars (David Bowie) – Light My Fire (The Doors) – London Calling (The Clash) – Long Time Gone (Crosby, Stills & Nash) – Long Train Runnin' (The Doobie Brothers) – The Look Of Love (Dusty Springfield) – Lust For Life (Iggy Pop) – Maggie May (Rod Stewart) – Make Me Smile (Come Up And See Me) (Steve Harley & Cockney Rebel) – Miss You (The Rolling Stones) – Moondance (Van Morrison) – More Than A Feeling (Boston) – Mustang Sally (Wilson Pickett) – New Kid In Town (The Eagles) – Oliver's Army (Elvis Costello) – Pale Blue Eyes (The Velvet Underground) – Perfect Day (Lou Reed) – Silence Is Golden (The Tremeloes) – Sloop John B (The Beach Boys) – Smoke On The Water (Deep Purple) – Space Oddity (David Bowie) – Start Me Up (The Rolling Stones) – Strange Kind Of Woman (Deep Purple) – Stuck In The Middle With You (Stealers Wheel) – Summer In The City (Lovin' Spoonful) – Sunny Afternoon (The Kinks) – Suzanne (Leonard Cohen) – Sweet Home Alabama (Lynyrd Skynyrd) – Tempted (The Squeeze) – Tequila Sunrise (The Eagles) – Turn Turn Turn (The Byrds) – Venus In Furs (The Velvet Underground) – We Gotta Get Out Of This Place (The Animals) – Whiter Shade Of Pale (Procol Harum) – Wuthering Heights (Kate Bush) – You're My Best Friend (Queen) - You've Got A Friend (James Taylor)

Essential Acoustic Strumalong
9808A   BK/CD   ISBN: 1-84328-335-2

All You Good Good People (Embrace) - American English (Idlewild) – The Drugs Don't Work (The Verve) – Grace (Supergrass) – Handbags And Gladrags (Stereophonics) – Hotel Yorba (The White Stripes) – Karma Police (Radiohead) – Love Burns (Black Rebel Motorcycle Club) – Poor Misguided Fool (Starsailor) – Powder Blue (Elbow) – Silent Sigh (Badly Drawn Boy) – Silent To The Dark (The Electric Soft Parade) – Tender (Blur) – There Goes The Fear (Doves) – Underdog (Save Me) (Turin Brakes)

Classic Acoustic Strumalong
9844A   BK/CD   ISBN: 1-84328-397-2

Alone Again Or (Love) – Another Brick In The Wall Part II (Pink Floyd) – Cocaine (Eric Clapton) – Get It On (T. Rex) – Handbags And Gladrags (Rod Stewart) – London Calling (The Clash) – Lust For Life (Iggy Pop) – Make Me Smile (Come Up And See Me) (Steve Harley & Cockney Rebel) – Mustang Sally (Wilson Pickett) – Perfect Day (Lou Reed) – Start Me Up (The Rolling Stones) – Stuck In The Middle With You (Stealers Wheel) – Sunny Afternoon (The Kinks) – Venus In Furs (Velvet Underground) – Whiter Shade Of Pale (Procol Harum)

Available now in all good music shops

Available Now
In all good music shops

MGARed 9699A ISBN1843282054

Papa Roach/Between Angels & Insects/Broken Home/Last Resort Puddle Of Mudd/Blurry/Control System Of A Down/ Chop Suey Hoobastank/Crawling In The Dark Incubus/Drive/Pardon Me/Wish You Were Here Lost Prophets/The Fake Sound Of Progress Sum 41/Fat Lip/In Too Deep Creed/Higher Nickleback/How You Remind Me/Too Bad Linkin Park/ In The End Staind/It's Been Awhile/Outside Slipknot/Left Behind/Wait & Bleed Jimmy Eat World/Middle Alien Ant Farm/ Movies/Smooth Criminal A/Nothing Blink 182/The Rock Show Limp Bizkit/Rollin' Disturbed/Shout 2000/Voices Marilyn Manson/Tainted Love

MGABlue 9705A ISBN1843282089

Starsailor/Alcoholic/Good Souls/Poor Misguided Fool Elbow/Asleep In The Back/Newborn/Powder Blue The Dandy Warhols/Bohemian Like You Feeder/Buck Rogers Vex Red/Can't Smile Turin Brakes/Emergency 72/Mind Over Money/Underdog (Save Me) The Electric Soft Parade/Empty At The End/Silent To The Dark The White Stripes/Fell In Love With A Girl/Hotel Yorba Radiohead/Knives Out/Pyramid Song Black Rebel Motorcycle Club/Love Burns/Spread Your Love Mercury Rev/Nite & Fog Haven/Say Something Hundred Reasons/Silver The Coral/Skeleton Key A/Starbucks The Music/The People Doves/There Goes The Fear Mull Historical Society/Watching Xanadu The Cooper Temple Clause/ Who Needs Enemies Idlewild/You Held The World In Your Arms

MGABlack 9798A ISBN1843286661

Foo Fighters/All My Life Drowning Pool/All Over Me Disturbed/Believe/Prayer/Remember Audioslave/ Cochise Hoobastank/ Crawling In The Dark Rob Zombie/Demon Speeding Puddle Of Mudd/Drift And Die/She Hates Me Crazy Town/Drowning Staind/Fade Raging Speedhorn/Fuck The Voodooman/The Hate Song Flaw/Get Up Again Ozzy Osbourne/Gets Me Through Ill Niño/God Save/Unreal Slipknot/My Plague/People = Shit Dry Kill Logic/Nightmare Marilyn Manson/Nobodies Kittie/Oracle/What I Always Wanted Slayer/ Perversions Of Pain Mudvayne/Severed Papa Roach/She Loves Me Not/Time And Time Again Filter/You Walk Away

MGAWhite 9856A ISBN1843284138

Badly Drawn Boy/All Possibilities JJ72/Always And Forever Mull Historical Society/Am I Wrong/The Final Arrears Turin Brakes/Average Man/Long Distance/Painkiller Richard Ashcroft/Buy It In Bottles The Mock Turtles/Can You Dig It British Sea Power/Carrion Blur/Crazy Beat/Out Of Time The Coral/Don't Think You're The First/Dreaming Of You The Flaming Lips/Fight Test/Yoshimi Battles The Pink Robots Starsailor/Four To The Floor/Silence Is Easy Longview/ Further The White Stripes/I Want To Be The Boy To Warm Your Mother's Heart/You've Got Her In Your Pocket The Bees/A Minha Menina Idlewild/A Modern Way Of Letting Go Johnny Cash/Personal Jesus Supergrass/Rush Hour Soul/ Seen The Light The Strokes/Someday Rooney/Stay Away Radiohead/There There Beth Orton/Thinking About Tomorrow The Libertines/Up The Bracket

MGAPurple 9855A ISBN184328412X

Simple Plan/Addicted Good Charlotte/The Anthem/Girls And Boys/Lifestyles Of The Rich And Famous The White Stripes/Ball And Biscuit/Seven Nation Army Stone Sour/ Bother/Inhale Evanescence/Bring Me To Life Radio 4/Eyes Wide Open The Kills/Fried My Little Brains OK Go/Get Over It A/Good Time Deftones/Hexagram/Minerva The Star Spangles/I Live For Speed/Stay Away From Me Nickelback/Learn The Hard Way/ Someday Foo Fighters/Low Kid Rock feat. Sheryl Crow/Picture Staind/Price To Play Sum41/ Still Waiting The Donnas/Take It Off/Who Invited You? The Used/The Taste Of Ink Nirvana/You Know You're Right